All Quilt Blocks Are Not Square

OTHER BOOKS AVAILABLE FROM CHILTON

Robbie Fanning, Series Editor

CONTEMPORARY QUILTING

Barbara Johannah's Crystal Piecing
The Complete Book of Machine Quilting, Second
    Edition, *by Robbie and Tony Fanning*
Contemporary Quilting Techniques, *by Pat Cairns*
Creative Triangles for Quilters, *by Janet B. Elwin*
Fast Patch, *by Anita Hallock*
Fourteen Easy Baby Quilts, *by Margaret Dittman*
Machine-Quilted Jackets, Vests, and Coats, *by Nancy
    Moore*
Pictorial Quilts, *by Carolyn Vosburg Hall*
Precision Pieced Quilts Using the Foundation Method,
    by Jane Hall and Dixie Haywood
Quick-Quilted Home Decor with Your Bernina, *by Jackie
    Dodson*
Quick-Quilted Home Decor with Your Sewing Machine,
    by Jackie Dodson
The Quilter's Guide to Rotary Cutting, *by Donna Poster*
Scrap Quilts Using Fast Patch, *by Anita Hallock*
Shirley Botsford's Daddy's Ties
Speed-Cut Quilts, *by Donna Poster*
Stitch 'n' Quilt, *by Kathleen Eaton*
Super Simple Quilts, *by Kathleen Eaton*
Teach Yourself Machine Piecing and Quilting, *by Debra
    Wagner*
Three-Dimensional Appliqué, *by Jodie Davis*
Three-Dimensional Pieced Quilts, *by Jodie Davis*

CRAFT KALEIDOSCOPE

Creating and Crafting Dolls, *by Eloise Piper and Mary
    Dilligan*
Fabric Crafts and Other Fun with Kids, *by Susan Parker
    Beck and Charlou Lunsford*
Fabric Painting Made Easy, *by Nancy Ward*
Jane Asher's Costume Book
Quick and Easy Ways with Ribbon, *by Ceci Johnson*
Learn Bearmaking, *by Judi Maddigan*
Soft Toys for Babies, *by Judi Maddigan*
Stamping Made Easy, *by Nancy Ward*
Too Hot To Handle? Potholders and How to Make
    Them, *by Doris L. Hoover*

CREATIVE MACHINE ARTS

ABCs of Serging, *by Tammy Young and Lori Bottom*
The Button Lover's Book, *by Marilyn Green*
Claire Shaeffer's Fabric Sewing Guide
The Complete Book of Machine Embroidery, *by Robbie
    and Tony Fanning*
Creative Nurseries Illustrated, *by Debra Terry and Juli
    Plooster*
Distinctive Serger Gifts and Crafts, *by Naomi Baker and
    Tammy Young*
Friendship Quilts by Hand and Machine, *by Carolyn
    Vosburg Hall*
Gail Brown's All-New Instant Interiors
Hold It! How to Sew Bags, Totes, Duffels, Pouches, and
    More, *by Nancy Restuccia*

How to Make Soft Jewelry, *by Jackie Dodson*
Innovative Serging, *by Gail Brown and Tammy Young*
Innovative Sewing, *by Gail Brown and Tammy Young*
Jan Saunders' Wardrobe Quick-Fixes
The New Creative Serging Illustrated, *by Pati Palmer, Gail
    Brown, and Sue Green*
Petite Pizzazz, *by Barb Griffin*
Putting on the Glitz, *by Sandra L. Hatch and Ann Boyce*
Quick Napkin Creations, *by Gail Brown*
Second Stitches: Recycle as You Sew, *by Susan Parker*
Serge a Simple Project, *by Tammy Young and Naomi Baker*
Serge Something Super for Your Kids, *by Cindy Cummins*
Sew Any Patch Pocket, *by Claire Shaeffer*
Sew Any Set-In Pocket, *by Claire Shaeffer*
Sew Sensational Gifts, *by Naomi Baker and Tammy Young*
Sewing and Collecting Vintage Fashions, *by Eileen
    MacIntosh*
Simply Serge Any Fabric, *by Naomi Baker and Tammy
    Young*
Soft Gardens: Make Flowers with Your Sewing
    Machine, *by Yvonne Perez-Collins*
The Stretch & Sew Guide to Sewing Knits, *by Ann Person*
Twenty Easy Machine-Made Rugs, *by Jackie Dodson*

KNOW YOUR SEWING MACHINE SERIES, *by Jackie Dodson*

Know Your Bernina, second edition
Know Your Brother, *with Jane Warnick*
Know Your New Home, *with Judi Cull and Vicki Lyn
    Hastings*
Know Your Pfaff, *with Audrey Griese*
Know Your Sewing Machine
Know Your Singer
Know Your Viking, *with Jan Saunders*
Know Your White, *with Jan Saunders*

KNOW YOUR SERGER SERIES, *by Tammy Young and Naomi Baker*

Know Your baby lock
Know Your Serger
Know Your White Superlock

STARWEAR

Dazzle, *by Linda Fry Kenzle*
Embellishments, *by Linda Fry Kenzle*
Make It Your Own, *by Lori Bottom and Ronda Chaney*
Mary Mulari's Garments with Style
Pattern-Free Fashions, *by Mary Lee Trees Cole*
Shirley Adams' Belt Bazaar
Sweatshirts with Style, *by Mary Mulari*

TEACH YOURSELF TO SEW BETTER, *by Jan Saunders*

A Step-by-Step Guide to Your Bernina
A Step-by-Step Guide to Your New Home
A Step-by-Step Guide to Your Sewing Machine
A Step-by-Step Guide to Your Viking

All Quilt Blocks Are Not Square

Innovative Piecing and Quilting of
Hexagons, Triangles, Curves, and More

Debra Wagner

Chilton Book Company
Radnor, Pennsylvania

Copyright © 1995 by Debra Wagner
All Rights Reserved

Published in Radnor, Pennsylvania 19089, by Chilton Book
Company

Designed by Anthony Jacobson
Manufactured in the United States of America

Library of Congress Cataloging in Publication Data
Wagner, Debra.
    All quilt blocks are not square : innovative piecing and quilting
of hexagons, triangles, curves, and more / Debra Wagner.
       p.   cm. — (Contemporary quilting)
    Includes bibliographical references and index.
    ISBN 0-8019-8643-5 (pbk.)
    1. Patchwork—Patterns.   2. Machine quilting—Patterns.
3. Patchwork quilts.   I. Title.   II. Series.
TT835.W3315   1995
746.46—dc20   95-33180
                                                  CIP

1 2 3 4 5 6 7 8 9 0   4 3 2 1 0 9 8 7 6 5

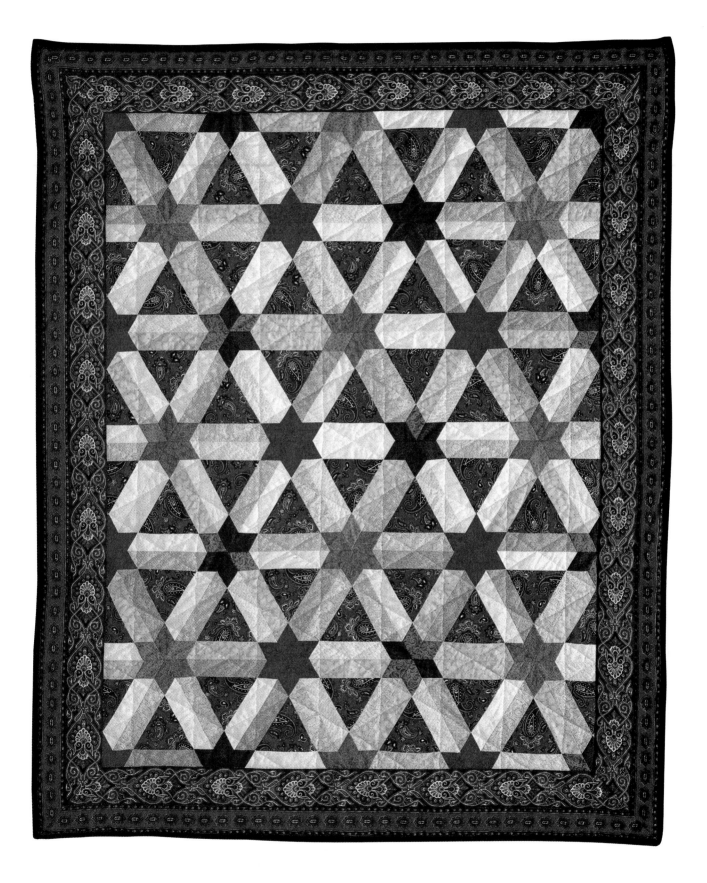

Contents

About this Book

This book has been designed for both the beginner and the experienced quilter. Twelve projects are presented in order of difficulty, interspersed with special hints and lessons. The projects provide patterns and ideas for interesting quilts, but the projects' main purpose is to illustrate the new and innovative methods. These techniques give you the skills to use more complex shapes in your quilts. They are also time-saving, going beyond the basics to make your quilting faster and more professional.

To help you find design, cutting, matching, and other hints and mini-lessons readily, they appear in a list immediately following.

The information in this book is presented in three parts. Part I, Innovative Piecing Patterns, includes instructions for 12 non-square piecing designs. The five chapters explain how to work with rectangles, triangles, curves, diamonds, and hexagons.

Part II, Machine Quilting, includes two chapters that will help improve your quilting skills and solve many common problems. This information updates and expands the techniques that appeared in my previous book, *Teach Yourself Machine Piecing and Quilting*. It addresses the intermediate and more experienced quilter. Chapter 7, Quilting Patterns for Borders, is just that—designs and ideas for you to use.

Quilter's Schoolhouse in Part III is a glossary of basic quiltmaking techniques. If you are making your first quilt, I recommend that you refer to Chapter 8 before you start your project. Anyone unfamiliar with quiltmaking, or who needs a brush-up on basic techniques, should find this chapter useful.

List of Special Hints and Lessons

Introduction

Not all quilt blocks are squares! There is a tempting array of hexagons, diamonds, triangles, curves, and whole-cloth quilts. As individuals, the non-square blocks are usually lackluster, but put a group together and these blocks become some of the most visually exciting designs. They tend to be graphic, sculptural, and often look three-dimensional. These wonderful "unsquare" shapes open a new world of design possibilities. They expand our sewing skills and challenge our ideas about what we can do with rotary cutters and sewing machines.

Traditionally, non-square blocks have been the province of hand quiltmakers. The patterns tend to require handling large amounts of fabric, and often require non-linear piecing that seems inconsistent with machine quiltmaking. Rather than oversimplify the designs or dismiss these great patterns as incompatible with machine quiltmaking, I developed my own techniques. I have taught and honed these techniques over the last six years. It is those techniques I want to share with you.

Think of this book as a technique book, not just a pattern book. Like my first book *Teach Yourself Machine Piecing and Quilting,* this book is designed as a workbook, a personally paced program that will take you step-by-step through new techniques using familiar patterns. I chose triangle-, diamond-, and hexagon-shaped blocks, with a few circle variations thrown in for excitement. I even included two unique square blocks. There are also directions for whole-cloth quilting, including marking and stitching, as well as some variations on quilt-as-you-go methods. I have chosen patterns that represent the widest range of techniques and skills. These same skills can be applied to other traditional patterns or to innovative and creative designs.

New and better techniques always wait to be discovered and integrated into our quilting repertoire. It is my sincere wish that these techniques and patterns help you create the quilts of your dreams.

PART I

INNOVATIVE PIECING PATTERNS

Introduction to Piecing Patterns

The patterns in this book are presented with complete directions and all the pattern pieces to make it easy for you to make any of the quilts illustrated. I've chosen patterns to appeal to all level of quiltmakers, beginner to experienced. I believe quilting, first and foremost, should be fun. I have designed the patterns and written the directions with that in mind. There is no math or geometry. No drafting patterns. The only difficult part is deciding which quilt to make. Each pattern has basic yardages, plus yardage alternatives. I hope you enjoy making the quilts and you learn a few new quilting techniques along the way.

Basic Instructions

▼ All pattern pieces have ¼" seam allowances, unless otherwise stated. The measurements for rotary-cut pieces include the ¼" seam allowance, unless otherwise noted.

▼ The yardages are based on a 44"/45" fabric with 42" usable. The yardages are generous to allow for shrinkage of the fabric and an occasional mistake in cutting.

▼ The cutting methods I use are speed methods. They do waste some fabric, but if time is money, speed methods more than pay for the lost fabric. But there are times that speed-cutting methods are not appropriate. I don't want to waste fabric that is in limited supply or extremely expensive. To use these fabrics to the best advantage, use traditional plastic templates. Then hand tracing and cutting won't waste one sliver of fabric.

Chapter 1

RECTANGLES

Endless T

Don't be misled by this innocent-looking square block. Endless T becomes a great non-square pattern. A single block looks like nothing, but stitch together 20 blocks and an overall pattern of capital Ts becomes clear. It is graphic…yet easy to piece, the perfect beginning pattern. The pieces are based on strip piecing combined with template cutting. The actual size of the strips and pieces is large, and the matches simple. Even the quilting pattern is a variation on Endless Ts. If you look closely, you will see the basic motif is a stylized T. It is twisted, flipped, and interwoven to make the quilting pattern. And of course, it is a continuous line design. This pattern is usually seen in just two colors, and the yardage is for that color arrangement. The yardage is also given for the rainbow variation wall quilt.

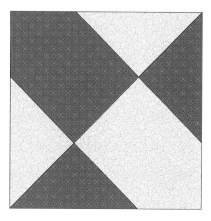

BLOCK SIZE

Approximately 6"

Pieces and corresponding strip sizes

Piece A1: 4" strip, the full width of the fabric

Piece A2: 3¼" strip, the full width of the fabric

Piece A3: 4" strip, the full width of the fabric

PIECING DIRECTIONS

1. Cut the number of 4" and 3¼" strips needed for the quilt size of your choice (see Endless T Information at the end of this section). Note that the blocks are made of two piece As and that the two sections are mirror images of each other. One piece A has a dark center (piece A2), the other a

light center. To obtain this effect you will be cutting light and dark strips in both widths.

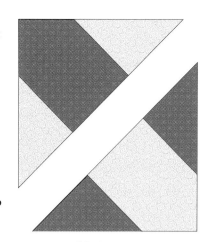

2. Sort the fabric into sets. Stack the light 3¼" strips and the dark 4" strips together to form a set of strips. Stack the remaining dark 3¼" strips and light 4" strips together to form a set of strips.

3. To make effective use of the fabric, the strips in each set will be sewn together in units. Beginning with a 4" strip on the outer edge, sew the strips together, alternating light and dark. Not only are you alternating color, you will also be alternating strip widths, first a 4" strip then a 3¼" strip. Press the seams toward the darker fabric. Repeat this step with second set of strips, to form two striped units of fabric.

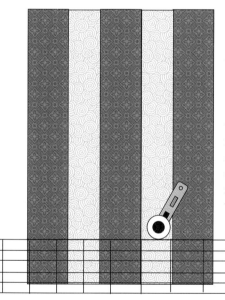

4. Rotary cut the units of striped fabric into 4¾" strips. Cut lengthwise across the stripes.

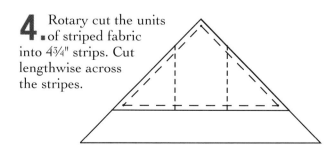

5. Make a clear plastic template of piece A. Mark the heavy dotted seam lines on the template.

6. Tape the template to a 45-degree triangle using transparent tape. Because the straight of grain is on the long side of the triangle, you must tape the template to the 90-degree angle.

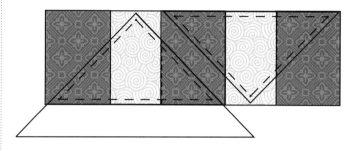

ROTARY CUTTING HINT
Using Plain Plexiglas Rulers: Substitute a clear, plain piece of ¼" Plexiglas for the plastic rotary ruler. I regularly use "clear" rulers for my rotary cutting. The unmarked Plexiglas allows a clear view of the template and fabric seams. Plus the clear Plexiglas is unharmed by tape. I am concerned that the transparent tape may damage the marks on my good rulers. To get your own "clear" rulers, look in the Yellow Pages for stores that specialize in Plexiglas cut to order. I have rulers made at my local plastic warehouse. They cut to fit any order and at a reasonable price. As basic sizes, I recommend a 6" × 12" rectangle and a 9" 45-degree triangle. See other chapters on more ways to use "clear" rulers.

---

7. To cut the triangle, place the ruler/template over the fabric strips. Line up the seams in the fabric with the lines on the template and line up the long edge of the template with the cut edge of the strips. All cuts will be on the bias. Flip the ruler to cut the next triangle. Continue across the strip. Cut the required pieces from both striped units.

8. Lay out two pieces to form the block. All the blocks will be identical.

9. Join the two triangles to form the blocks. Use "keying" to match the intersecting seams (see Part III, Quilter's Schoolhouse). Press open the seam. Press carefully, using steam. The block edges are bias and can stretch. Move the iron in an up-and-down motion; do not drag it across the block.

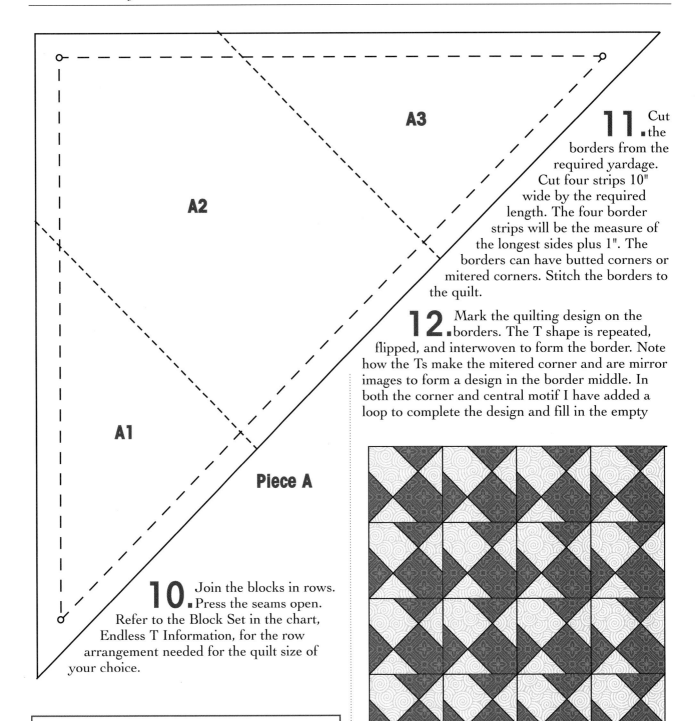

A3

A2

A1

Piece A

11. Cut the borders from the required yardage. Cut four strips 10" wide by the required length. The four border strips will be the measure of the longest sides plus 1". The borders can have butted corners or mitered corners. Stitch the borders to the quilt.

12. Mark the quilting design on the borders. The T shape is repeated, flipped, and interwoven to form the border. Note how the Ts make the mitered corner and are mirror images to form a design in the border middle. In both the corner and central motif I have added a loop to complete the design and fill in the empty

10. Join the blocks in rows. Press the seams open. Refer to the Block Set in the chart, Endless T Information, for the row arrangement needed for the quilt size of your choice.

ROTARY CUTTING HINT

Preventing Rulers from Slipping: To help hold your template and ruler in place on the fabric while you rotary cut, use an old hand-piecing trick. Adhere small squares of adhesive-backed sandpaper to the wrong side of the plastic template. The coarse sandpaper gives the template "tooth," the ability to stick to the fabrics, and prevents the ruler from slipping while you cut. You can get self-stick sandpaper at a hardware store or lumber yard. It is commonly sold in disk shapes for use on orbital sanders.

DESIGN HINT

Fitting a Quilting Design to a Border: To fit the motifs to the quilt, it is important that you draw the corners first, then the middle motif, before filling in the rest of the border. Any discrepancy in the pattern is less noticeable in the body of the border rather than the corners or central motifs. As in all quilting designs it is impossible for one size motif to perfectly fit the varying measurements of the quilt sides. Check the number of motifs recommended for the border. As an example, the twin size requires ten repeats on the 68" border. The two corner repeats and the two mirror image repeats in the center total four repeats, leaving six repeats. There will be three repeats from corner to center motif in each half of the border. Measure the distance between the corner motif and center motif. Divide that measure by the number of repeats. In the example, you will divide the measure by three. Lightly mark the three divisions. Then fit the repeats into the allotted space. This way they will be evenly compacted or stretched across the entire border.

The quilting pattern for the body of the quilt is a variation of continuous curve quilting. It is not marked on the fabric because it follows the piecing pattern. I recommend that you stitch in the darker colored Ts, especially on the Rainbow Variation. It is impossible to illustrate and number every one of the stitching lines for the entire quilt. The illustration shows a small section of the stitching. Basically the Ts are stitched in rows. Each row is stitched in two directions. One half of the row starts at the top and moves toward the bottom. The second half of the row completes the Ts from the bottom to the top.

Endless T Information

	Crib	Twin	Double	Queen	King
Finished size	42" × 55"	68" × 92"	80" × 98"	86" × 104"	104" × 104"
Border width	10"	10"	10"	10"	10"
Block set	4 × 6	8 × 12	10 × 13	11 × 14	14 × 14
Number of blocks	24	96	130	154	196
Number of quilting repeats on a side	6 & 8	10 & 14	12 & 16*	14* & 16	16 &16
* use smaller version of quilting pattern					
Amount of fabric required (in yards)					
Light color	¾	2½	3⅝	4¼	5¼
Dark color and border	2½	5¼	6⅜	7¼	8⅜
Backing	1⅝	5¼	5⅝	9 of 42″ (6 of 44″)	9
Bias binding	½	¾	⅞	⅞	1
Cutting Guide					
Blocks					
Light color, 4" strips	4	13	19	21	26
Light color, 3.25" strips	3	12	18	20	25
Dark color, 4" strips	4	13	19	21	26
Dark color, 3.25" strips	3	12	18	20	25
Total pieces (each strip unit)	24	96	130	154	196
Borders (length)	56"	93"	99"	105"	105"

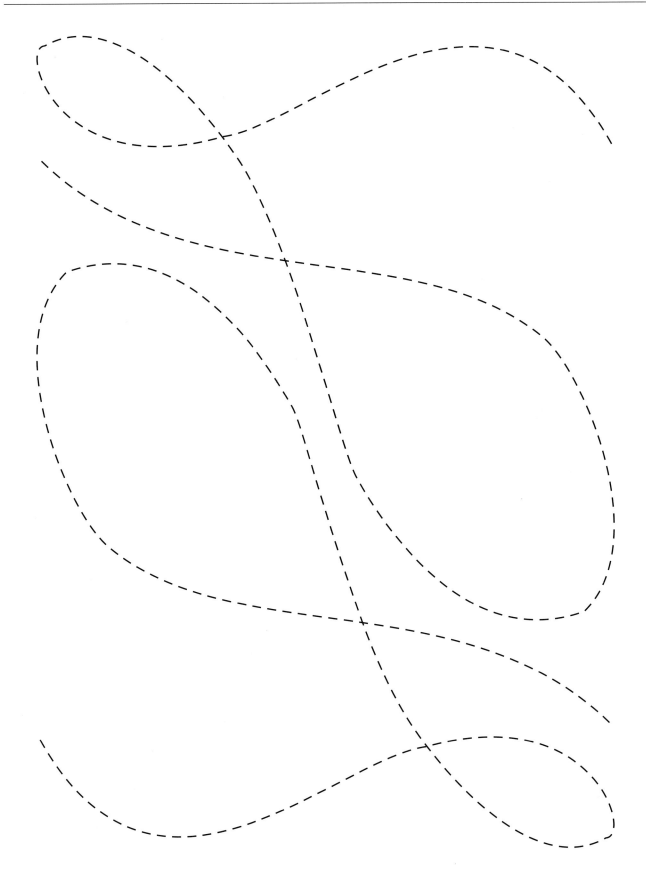

space that resulted from joining the basic T patterns. I have mathematically designed the pattern to fit as closely as possible to all the quilts, but you will have to make minor adjustments as you mark the quilt. The designs may need to be compacted or expanded to fit the space. See the chart, Endless T

Information, for the number of motifs recommended for each side of the quilt.

13. Stitch the backing together and prepare the quilt for quilting. Layer and baste the quilt.

14. Quilt the quilt and finish with ½"-wide French bias binding.

Endless T Rainbow

This color variation of Endless T uses bright crayon colors with black. The wall hanging is finished with a rod pocket and prairie points.

	T body blocks		T top blocks
Color Set A	red	+	orange
Color Set B	orange	+	yellow
Color Set C	yellow	+	green
Color Set D	green	+	blue
Color Set E	blue	+	purple
Color Set F	purple	+	red

Endless T Rainbow Information

Finished size	50" × 62"
Border width	10"
Block set	5 × 7
Total blocks	35
Number of quilting repeats on a side	8* × 10*
* use smaller version of quilting pattern	
Number of prairie points per side	Crayon Colors 13 × 16
	Black 12 × 15

Amount of fabric required (in yards)

Color (red, orange, yellow, green, blue, purple) blocks & prairie points (each color)	½
Black blocks, borders, & prairie points	5
Backing	3½
Binding (should match the backing)	½
Rod pocket	12"

Cutting Guide

Red, orange, yellow, green, blue, purple, 4" strips (each color)	2
Red, orange, yellow, green, blue, purple, 3¼" strips (each color)	1
Black, 4" strips	12
Black, 3¼" strips	6

PIECING DIRECTIONS

1. Cut the required strips. Piece the strips into units of three. Six units will be made of two matching 4" color strips with a center strip that is 3¼" black. The other six units will be the opposite: Two 4" black strips with a center strip of 3¼" color.

2. Cut the triangle-shaped half blocks following steps 4 through 7 under Endless T, in the previous section. Only six piece As are needed from each unit of strips.

3. To make the rainbow arrangement of colors, the colored half blocks need to be stitched in a certain color group. To make it easier, I refer to the triangles with colored center strips as the T body blocks. The triangles with two colored ends are called the T top blocks. Sew the blocks together in the following sets.

4. Stitch the blocks following step 9 under Endless T. Lay the blocks out as indicated.

5. Continue constructing the quilt following steps 10 through 13 under Endless T.

6. Cut the prairie points. Rotary cut 4½" squares. Cut 10 squares of each color and 60 squares of black. To make the prairie point, fold the square in half diagonally. Press. Fold the resulting triangle in half again, lining up the raw edges. Press.

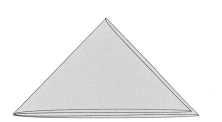

7. This quilt uses a double row of points. The top row is made of the colored points. The back row is made of black. First place the colored points around the quilt edges. Place them on the right side of the quilt. Line up the raw edges of the prairie point with the raw edges of the quilt top. Evenly distribute the points around the quilt. The points may have to be slightly over-lapped to fit the length. Refer to the chart Endless T Information for the recom-mended number of prairie points on each side of the quilt. For the best mix of col-ors, position them in a color sequence of red, orange, yellow, green, blue, purple. Pin them securely and then machine baste. Next position the black points over the color. The point of the black prairie point should fall between the points of the colored prairie points. Pin in place.

8. Stitch the prairie points along the quilt edges. Use a ¼" seam allowance.

9. Add the rod pocket. Cut one strip 12" wide. Hem the 12" ends with a small hem. Fold the rod pocket in half lengthwise, right sides out. Center the pocket on the quilt back. Line up the raw edges of the rod pocket with the top of the quilt. Machine baste the pocket in place with a ¼" seam.

10. Cut the bias binding 1½" wide. Stitch a mock binding. Position the binding strip on top of the prairie points. Lining up the raw edges, stitch with a generous ¼" seam allowance.

11. Turn the binding to the quilt back and hand stitch in place. Hand blindstitch the lower edge of pocket to the quilt back.

Chapter 2

TRIANGLES

Stars and Bars

Stars and Bars is a perfect intermediate pattern. The large pieces are easy to cut using a rotary cutter. I have chosen a strip-piecing method that combines two pieces, the diamond for the star and the bar. Cutting one piece will yield two! Plus, it excludes the sometimes confusing step of stitching the diamond to the bar. In this pattern the triangle-shaped blocks form six-pointed stars in the block corners. This makes the matches slightly more difficult than the *Continuous T,* but well in the range of a novice quilter. The charm of this pattern is in the striking repeat of the piecing and the strong color choices. There are dozens of color possibilities, from a simple two-color version to multicolored versions that appear three-dimensional. My quilt is the mini *Stars and Bars* in a five-color version inspired by an 1880s quilt. Notice the blocks are arranged to form three different colored stars, while the bars are made from an assortment of scrap fabrics. To make it easier for you to design your own version of *Stars and Bars*, the yardage is given separately for the bars, stars, and triangles.

BLOCK SIZE

10½" along the edge of the triangle and 9" high

Pieces and corresponding strip sizes

Piece A: 2" strips, the full width of the fabric—each strip yields about 16 pieces

Piece B: 5¼" strips, the full width of the fabric—each strip yields about 13 pieces

Piece C: 6¾" strips, the full width of the fabric—each strip yields about 16 pieces

PIECING DIRECTIONS

1. Study the photographs to help you choose a color arrangement. The yardage in the chart, *Stars and Bars* Information, at the end of this section, is given for a single color and for my variation of three color stars. Determine the color placement you like before buying the fabric or cutting the strips needed for the quilt size of your choice. *You do not need both sets of yardage.* Make sure you buy the correct amount of fabric for the quilt you are planning.

2. Cut the number of strips needed for the quilt size of your choice. Sort the fabric into sets according to the fabric width.

3. To make the stars and bars, strips A and C will be stitched together and the pieces cut as a unit. To effectively use the fabric, the strips for the stars (piece A) and bars (piece C) will be sewn off-set 2½". Prepare to sew the two strips together. Place a star strip (A) and a bar strip (B) right sides together. Slide the star strip 2½" lower than the bar strip and pin. Sew with the bar strip (B) on top. Complete all strip sets. Press open the seams.

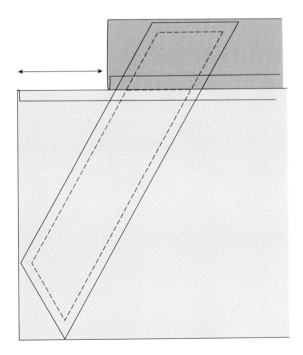

4. Cut the offset edges of the strips to 60 degrees: Place a 60-degree triangle as illustrated, a straight edge of the triangle along the bottom of the strips, and the angled edge across both strips of fabric and bisecting the offset seam. Cut along this edge.

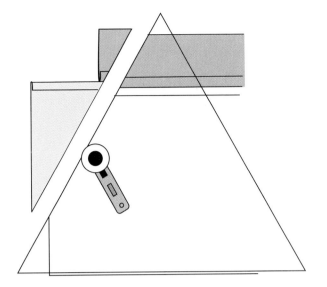

5. Make a clear plastic template of piece A/C. Mark the dotted seamline on the template. Tape the template to a 60-degree triangle using transparent tape. Tape as illustrated. Place the ruler/template on the A/C strips. For every piece you cut, you will be making two cuts with the rotary cutter. One cut is the strip width; the other cut makes the 60-degree strip end.

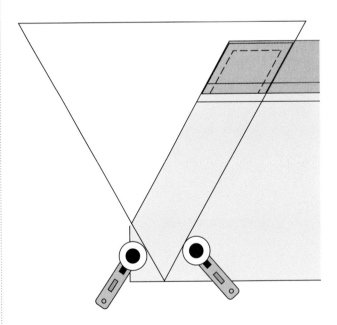

ROTARY CUTTING HINT

Using a 60-degree Plexiglas Triangle: 60-degree rulers and triangles can be purchased from quilting stores and office supply stores. Or you can have your own made at a Plexiglas retailer. I have both a 12" 60-degree triangle and a 24" x 6" Plexiglas piece that has been trimmed with a 60-degree angle on one end.

6. Make a paper or plastic template of triangle B. Tape the template to the 60-degree triangle using transparent tape. Tape as illustrated.

7. To cut the triangle, place the ruler/template over the fabric strips. Line up the edge of the template with the cut edge of the strip. All cuts will be on the bias. Flip the ruler to cut the next triangle. Continue across the strip.

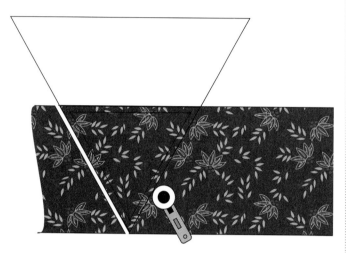

8. Lay out the four pieces to form the block: three piece A/Cs and one piece B. To make the three color stars requires two basic block layouts. The blocks are sewn identically, but the color sequence is altered. Half the blocks are made in each sequence. The color sequences in the blocks are mirror images. Moving clockwise around one block the colors are color 1, color 2, and color 3. For the other block the clockwise color sequence is color 1, color 3, and color 2 (see at right). As a piecing tip, notice all the top/even numbered blocks in the rows are one color sequence. The bottom/odd numbered blocks in the rows are the alternate color sequence. The blocks are turned to set the correct corners

together, but the blocks in the upper and lower portions of the rows are mirror images (see page 16).

MATCHING HINT

Needle Down Start: Needle down starts are the perfect way to line up irregular pieces and work with most seams. It is extremely important the pieces have been accurately rotary cut. Inaccurate cutting will negatively affect the results.

On the machine, raise the presser foot and lower the needle into the needle plate. It doesn't have to be completely lowered; just the tip of the needle will suffice. (Use the Needle Down feature on your machine for even faster starts.) Place the first piece right side up under the foot. Line up the ¼" seam line and slide the piece toward the needle until it touches the needle. Now place the second piece right side down on top of the first. Line up the ¼" seam lines and slide the piece until the edge is against the needle. Lower the presser foot and sew. This will give you the perfect start every time.

Sew from the edge of the block to about halfway—do not complete the entire seam. Finger press open a short section of this seam. Take care not to stretch or pleat the unsewn sections.

---

9. The first piece A/C is joined to triangle B with a partial seam. This is the only partial seam in this block. It is important that piece A/C is correctly lined up with triangle B. The best way to stitch this seam is with the triangle on the *bottom*, and the

A/C piece on top, right sides together. It can be confusing trying to correctly line up the pieces. There are a number of ways to solve the problem, but my favorite uses the needle on the sewing machine and the ¼" seam allowance. It is the "needle down start." The key to this perfect match is at the end of the seam line.

10. The second piece of A/C is joined to the triangle with a complete seam that is sewn the entire length of A/C. There is a match where the diamond in the strip matches the triangle in the block center. You can mark this with a stab pin, but it is very difficult to locate the exact matching point without match dots. There is a simple and very accurate method that uses the seam allowance "flags" from the previous seam.

11. Press open the seam. Add the third piece A/C as you did for the previous piece and press open the seam.

12. Finish stitching the basic block by completing the seam for the first piece. Press open the seam.

13. Lay out the blocks to form the quilt. The blocks are laid out in strips of triangles. For my color version, one color sequence makes the bottom blocks in every row, the other color sequence makes the upper blocks in every row. Refer to the Block Set in the *Stars and Bars* Information that follows, for the row arrangement needed for the quilt size of your choice.

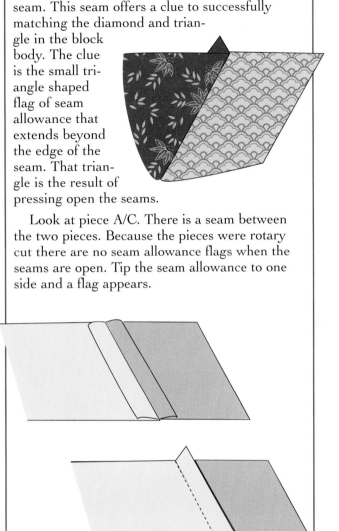

MATCHING HINT

Flag Matches: Notice the previous stitched seam. This seam offers a clue to successfully matching the diamond and triangle in the block body. The clue is the small triangle shaped flag of seam allowance that extends beyond the edge of the seam. That triangle is the result of pressing open the seams.

Look at piece A/C. There is a seam between the two pieces. Because the pieces were rotary cut there are no seam allowance flags when the seams are open. Tip the seam allowance to one side and a flag appears.

Place the flag from piece A/C over the flag from the previous stitched seam. Pin the match, pinning only the block, not the seam allowances. Return the seam allowance to open. This will be sewn as an open seam.

Stitch the seam. Remember to use the needle down start when you begin sewing. Both the seam beginning and end should have a small triangle extending beyond the upper piece, as the seam beginning had in the previous step. Depending on your level of accuracy, you can use the needle down start and flags for all the matches in this block and completely omit stab pinning the matches.

14. Join the triangles to make the rows. Use the flags (or modified key match) to match the star seams and securely pin the matches. Press open the seams.

15. Join the rows to make the quilt. Use the flags (or modified key match) to match the star seams and stab pins for the star center. Press open the seams.

PIECING HINT

Perfect Star Centers: It is a common problem when sewing stars for the stitching to be off in the points in the star center. To correct the problem, always sew a thread width or two to the right of the center match. It will look as if you've missed the match and the 1/4" seam line from the wrong side. This tiny variation of the 1/4" seam will not affect the finished quilt, but it will ensure sharp center points.

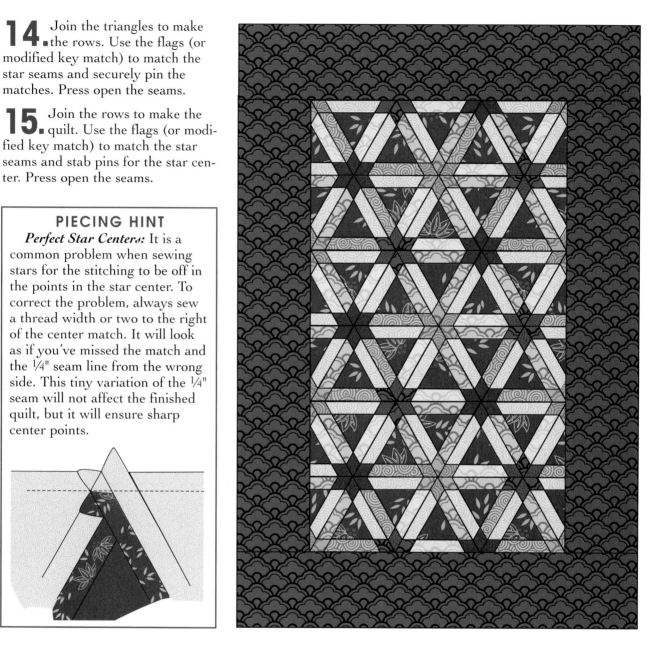

16. Cut the borders from the required yardage. Cut four strips 10" wide by the recommended length. The four border strips will be the measure of the longest sides plus 1". The borders should be made with butted borders to fit the quilting pattern.

17. Straighten the edge of the quilt body and stitch the borders in place.

18. Mark the quilting design on the borders. Choose a border pattern from the quilt pattern selection located in the back of the book.

PIECING HINT

Straightening Irregular Edges: It is easy to see that it is impossible to sew straight borders to an irregular edge. Stars and Bars offers a perfect chance to show you how to easily straighten any irregular edge without having to make half or mirror image partial blocks. You might choose to straighten the irregular edge so that you can add a border or make the binding easier. Later chapters will give step-by-step instructions on how to bind odd angles if you prefer to finish your quilt without the borders and retain the uneven edges.

To straighten the edges requires cutting the edge blocks. Don't be mislead into thinking that you simply cut the block in half. I know it seems logical that cutting a block in half would let you use one half on each side of the quilt. It appears so neat. It would prevent wasting fabric and making unnecessary blocks. But, no matter how right it looks, for most blocks it *won't* work. The partial blocks on the quilt edge must be cut ¼" beyond the exact center of the block to allow for a seam allowance. The best time to straighten the edge is after the quilt body is completed. Use a 24" ruler and place the ¼" mark of the ruler over the block centers. In this quilt the center falls through the points of the diamond and triangle. Use a fabric marker to mark along the ruler edge. (To be on the safe side, I don't recommend novice quilters cut the blocks until after the border is stitched in place. The experienced quilter may choose to rotary cut the quilt edge as it is measured.)

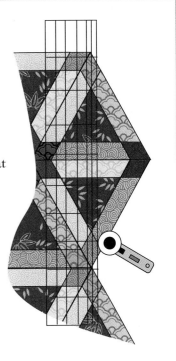

The quilting patterns for the body of the quilt are a variation of grid quilting. The lines are not marked on the quilt top because they follow the piecing pattern.

19. Stitch the backing together and prepare the quilt for quilting. Layer and baste the quilt.

20. Quilt the quilt and finish with ½"-wide French bias binding.

Stars and Bars Information

	Crib	Twin	Double	Queen	King
Finished size	41" × 56"	72" × 92"	83" × 101"	93" × 101"	114" × 114"
Border width	10"	10"	10"	10"	10"
Block set	5 × 4	11 × 8	13 × 9	15 × 9	19 × 11
Number of blocks	20	88	117	135	209
Amount of fabric required (in yards)					
Stars					
One color	⅜	¾	1¼	1½	2⅛
Three color (each color)	⅛	⅜	½	½	⅞
Bars					
For one color stars	⅞	2⅝	4	4¾	7⅛
For three color stars	1¼	3½	4	4¾	7½
Center triangles	⅓	1¼	1¾	2	2⅞
Borders with butted corners	1¼	2⅛	2⅓	2¾	3⅓
Backing	1⅝	5¼	5¾	5¾	6¾
Bias binding	½	⅞	⅞	⅞	1⅛

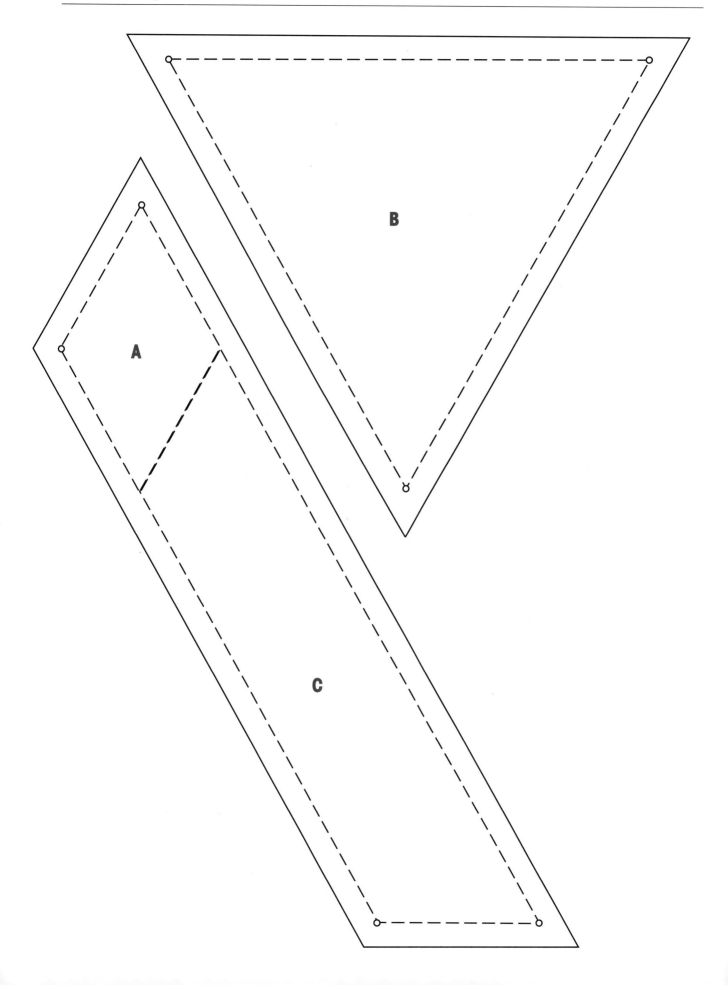

Stars and Bars Information (continued)					
	Crib	**Twin**	**Double**	**Queen**	**King**
Cutting guide					
Stars					
One color, 2" strips, A	4	13	21	24	37
Each of three colors, 2" strips, A	2	6	7	8	13
Bars					
For one-color stars, 6¾" strips, C	4	13	21	24	37
For three-color stars, 6¾" strips, C	6	18	21	24	39
Total pieces A/C for one color stars	60	264	351	405	627
Total pieces A/C for each color of three color stars	30	132	177	204	315
Triangle center, 5¼" strips B	2	8	11	13	19
Total pieces B	20	88	117	135	209

Stars and Bars Mini Quilt

This smaller version of *Stars and Bars* is great for a wall hanging. Its smaller pieces show the pattern off to its best advantage. At 36" × 38" it requires a surprising 54 blocks! It is beautiful as a scrap quilt. I used assorted beige, red, teal, and gold fabrics for the stars and bars, and used a paisley print as the companion for the triangles.

PIECING DIRECTIONS

1. Follow steps 1 and 2 under *Stars and Bars* in the previous section.

2. To make the stars and bars, strips A and C will be stitched together and the pieces cut as a unit. To effectively use the fabric, the strips for the stars (piece A) and bars (piece C) will be offset by 1¾" then sewn. Prepare to sew the two strips together. Place a star strip (A) on top of the bar strip (B), right sides together. Slide the star strip 1¾" lower than the bar strip. Join the two strips together. Sew all the strips together. Press open the seams.

3. Complete the quilt using steps 4 through 17 under *Stars and Bars*.

4. Quilt the wall hanging and add the rod pocket. Cut one strip 12" × 36". Hem the 12" ends with a small hem. Fold the rod pocket in half lengthwise, right sides out.

Stars and Bars Mini Quilt Information	
Finished size	36" × 38"
Border width	4"
Block set	9 × 6
Number of blocks	54
Amount of Fabric Required (in yards)	
Stars, each of three colors	¼
Bars	1⅜
Center triangle	½
Borders	1⅛
Backing and Rod Pocket	1½
Bias binding	½
Cutting Guide	
Stars	
For each of three colors, 1½" strips A	3
Bars	
4¾" strips C	9
Total pieces A/C	162
Triangle center	
3¾" strips B	4
Total pieces B	54

Center the pocket on the quilt back. Line up the raw edges of the rod pocket with the top of the quilt. Machine baste the pocket in place with a ¼" seam.

5. Bind with ½"-wide French bias binding. Hand blindstitch the lower edge of pocket to the quilt back.

DESIGN HINT

Using Scrap Fabrics in Strip-Pieced Patterns: It's very easy to substitute assorted fabrics for yardage for any of the quilts in this book. The only requirement is that the fabric be the full 42"/44" width. I designed the directions to give you the number and widths of all the strips needed for every size quilt. The Cutting Guide in the chart that follows lists the number of strips and the width needed for each piece in the block. In the *Stars and Bars* Mini Quilt, there are three strips of each color needed for the stars. I used three different pieces of red, three different pieces of teal, and three different pieces of gold. I used the same approach for the bars. Nine strips are required and I cut my strips from my beige "stash" using numerous fabrics.

You can be even more creative in using your scraps by piecing each strip. For example, I could have used two pieces of red prints, each 21"–22" by 1½". Together they measure 42"–44" × 1½", enough for one star strip. Just consider these two strips as a single fabric 42"– 44" wide. You may have to cut an extra strip or two, because this method wastes fabric and the yardage given in the *Stars and Bars* Mini Quilt Information that follows, will be short. Of course, that isn't a problem when using scraps; just add a few more pieces to the assortment.

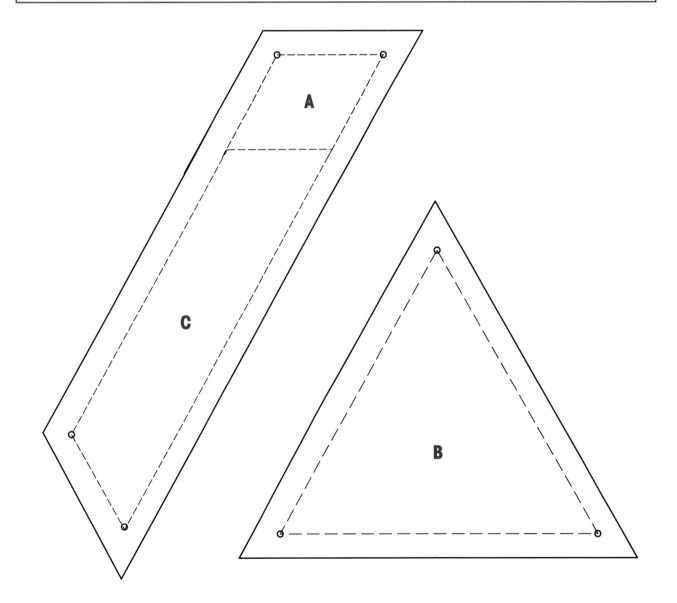

Orange Peel

Orange Peel is frequently based on a square, but this exceptional variation is based on a triangle. The quilt that inspired this pattern was made in the 1930s using an extensive collection of feed-sack fabrics. The colors were muted and the prints confusing, almost totally concealing the wonderfully graphic pattern. To me, it seemed the striking pattern required a more vibrant color range. The orange and gold colors in my sample were inspired by a late 1800s traditional *Orange Peel*. In this variation the blocks alternate in color. Half the blocks are light with dark edges, while the other half are dark with light edges. The whole effect is a riveting, three-dimensional pattern reminiscent of Op-Art. There are two pieces to this quilt, the ellipse and the triangle. The curves are easy gentle curves and the block set simple. The block set is identical to *Stars and Bars*, using the 60-degree triangle block. To make the blocks easier to piece, the ellipse doesn't touch the corner of the block. This reduces the number of points that converge at each corner and adds to the optical illusion by making each ellipse appear to be floating on the background. There are a number of ways to finish the quilt edge. You may choose to finish the quilt
with the uneven
edge, or cut the
completed blocks to
make a straight edge,
like the methods used
with *Stars and Bars*. The
yardage and directions are
for the partial blocks and
narrow borders shown in the
sample. To add to the riotous
colors, the quilt is finished with a
contrasting binding.

BLOCK SIZE

7" along the edge of the triangle and 6" high

Pieces and corresponding strip sizes

Pieces A and A1 (triangles and half triangles): 7" strip width—the full width yields 9 full pieces and two half pieces

Piece B (ellipse): 7" strip—the full width yields 30 full pieces

PIECING DIRECTIONS

1. Cut the number of strips required for the quilt size of your choice.

2. Make the pattern templates. Use paper or plastic for scissor-cut pieces. Use heavy template plastic or Plexiglas for rotary templates. This pattern is suited to rotary cutting, but requires specific templates.

3. Cut the pieces for the strips as illustrated. Refer to the chart, *Orange Peel* Information, for the required number of pieces in each color. As you cut the pieces, take care to cut the correct number and color of each piece. The most crucial are the two half pieces, A1. The two half pieces are cut from the right and left edge of the strip. To cut them will require flipping the template. That is correct. The two pieces are mirror images, one cut with the template right side up, the other cut with the template wrong side up. They make the left and right hand sides of the quilt. Also remember half the blocks are dark with light ellipses. The other half of the blocks are light with dark ellipses.

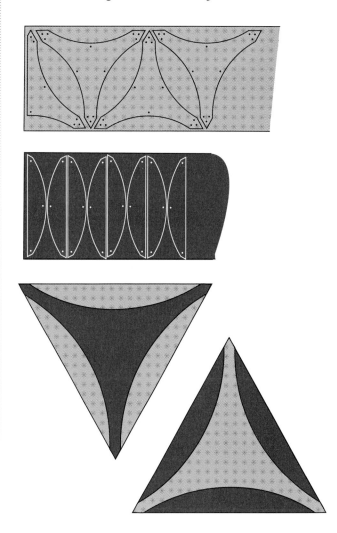

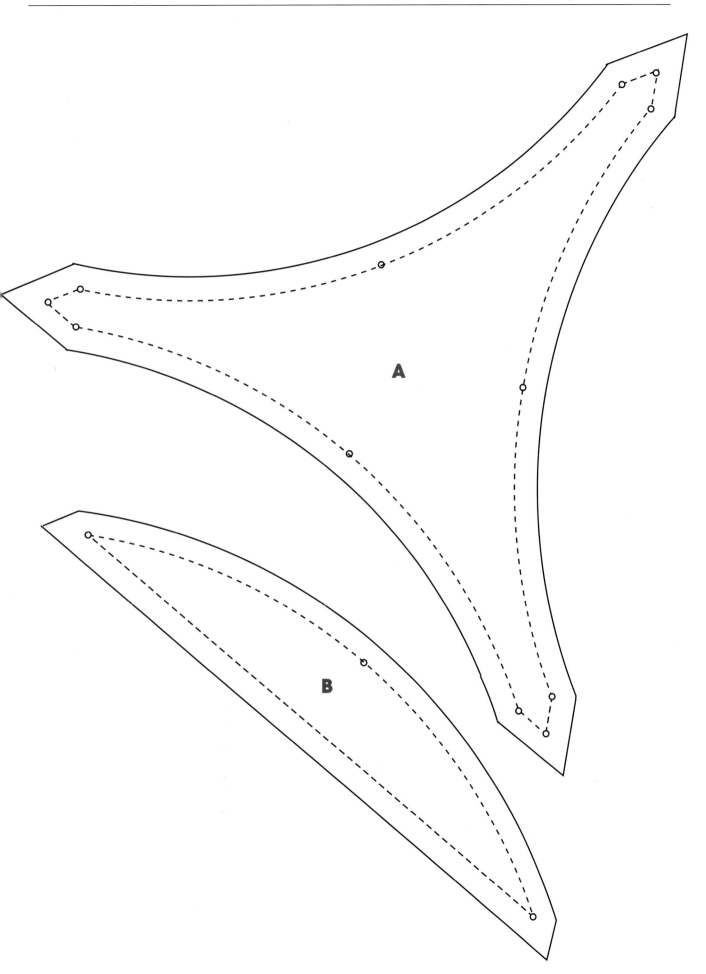

A1
(half pattern)

7. After stitching the three ellipses, press open the seams. Do not press the seams until all the pieces are stitched in place. The unstitched bias edges and narrow points of the triangle are fragile and can be stretched by overzealous pressing.

4. The beginner should mark the midpoints of the triangle and ellipse seams to help stitch the curves. The advanced quilter doesn't need to mark the matching dots.

8. Construct the half blocks, stitching two ellipses to each block. Take special care when using solid colors. The lack of right and wrong sides to the fabric can be confusing. Reversing the fabric will result in ends that match instead of mirror-image ends. To help reduce the confusion, make the half blocks in sets of two. Always make one left side and one right side for each row. Press open the seams. Trim the ellipse as shown.

5. Pin an ellipse to the triangle. Line up the pieces as illustrated. Notice how the pattern for the ellipse has clipped corners to facilitate setting the ellipse. Pin both ends of the ellipse to the triangle. Beginners should pin the midpoint.

9. Lay out the blocks to form the quilt. The blocks are laid out in strips of triangles with the half blocks making the straight edges. The blocks alternate in color. To make the quilt easier to lay out, note all the odd rows are identical, and all the even rows are identical. Refer to Block Set in the chart, *Orange Peel* Information, for the row arrangement needed for the quilt size of your choice.

6. The curves in *Orange Peel* are simple to piece for two reasons. First, the curve is so flat, it is almost a straight line. Second, the grainlines on the triangle part of the seam are predominately bias (two seams in each triangle are bias, while one is straight of grain). Sew with the ellipse down and the triangle on top. Start stitching at the edge of the fabric. To stitch the curve successfully, slightly stretch the triangle edge to match the ellipse. Individually pin and stitch each of the three ellipses in place.

MATCHING HINT

Matching Ellipse Seams: Matching the ellipse seams is surprisingly simple. To help match the seams, use a modified keyed match. Tip the seam allowances on the ellipse seams to the darker side. Because the blocks are in alternating colors, one seam will be tipped to the triangle, the other toward the ellipse. Slide the seams together. They will fit perfectly. Secure the match by pinning the block, *not* the seam allowance. Then open the seams. That way the seam allowances can be stitched as open seams. Keying makes an easy perfect match, and the open seams result in a flat block with reduced amount of fabric in the intricate matches.

10.
Join the triangles to make the blocks. To make matching the ellipses easier, use a modified key match. Press open all seams as you join the triangles.

11.
Join the rows to make the quilt. Use the stab pin match to match the triangle points. Press open the seams.

Orange Peel **Information**					
	Crib	**Twin**	**Double**	**Queen**	**King**
Finished size	39 × 52	64 × 88	81 × 94	89 × 100	116 × 118
Border width	2"	2"	2"	2"	2"
Block set	9 × 8	17 × 14	21 × 15	23 × 16	31 × 19
Total whole blocks	72	238	315	368	589
Total half blocks	16	28	30	32	38
Amount of fabric required (in yards)					
Blocks					
Light fabrics	2	5⅜	7	8⅛	12⅝
Dark fabrics	2	5⅜	7	8⅛	12⅝
Border with butted corners					
(cross-grain cut with bias joins)	½	¾	¾	⅞	1⅛
Backing	1½	5	5½	9	10⅛
Bias binding (for bordered straight					
edge version)	½	¾	⅞	⅞	1⅛
Cutting Guide					
Triangles, A and A1, 7" strips					
(for each color)	4	14	18	21	33
Total piece A, each color	36	119	158	184	295
Total piece A1, each color	8	14	16	16	19
Ellipse, B, 7" strips (each color)	4	12	16	19	30
Total piece B, each color	124	385	506	584	923
Border, cross-grain, 2½" strips	5	8	9	10	12

14. The quilting pattern for the body of the quilt is a variation of continuous curve quilting. It is not marked on the fabric because it follows the piecing pattern. It is impossible to illustrate and number every one of the stitching lines for the entire quilt. The illustration shows a small section of the stitching. The pattern is stitched in the triangles, not in the smaller melon-shaped pieces. Each row of triangles is stitched in two directions. One half of the row starts at the top and moves toward the bottom. The second half of the row completes the triangles from the bottom to the top.

15. Stitch the backing together and prepare the quilt for quilting. Layer and baste the quilt.

16. Quilt the quilt and finish with ½"-wide French bias binding.

12. Cut the borders from the required yardage. These borders are cut crossgrain because they are so narrow. Cross cutting saves on yardage but does require frequent piecing of the border. Cut the number of strips required for the quilt of your choice. The strips are 2½" by 42" (or the actual width of the fabric). Cut off the selvage from both ends of the strips and join with a straight seam. Press open the seam allowances. From the long strip cut two lengths that match the longest sides of the quilt body. Join to the quilt. Cut two lengths that match the shortest sides of the quilt *plus* the measure of the first two borders. Stitch to the short sides of the quilt.

13. Mark the quilting design on the borders. Choose a border pattern from the quilt pattern selection located in the back of the book.

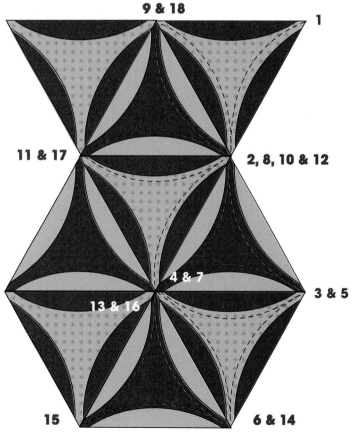

Chapter 3
CURVES

Candy Swirl

Candy Swirl is a stunning curved pattern from the early 1900s. Originally, the pattern was simply named *Swirl*. Its design reminds me of saltwater taffy. That's why I named it *Candy Swirl*. This pattern is loaded with surprises, from the piecing to the sets. Its eye-popping effect belies the simple block it is based on. There is only one pattern piece to this block, and only four pieces to make a block. The block is not for the beginner, but surprisingly is well within the reach of the intermediate quilter. The blocks are simple squares and easy to set, whether straight or diagonal. The only difficult parts of the block are the curves. The curves are tight and require accurate stitching for the block to finish square. This block is an excellent place to hone your curved-seam techniques. I'll give you extra hints that will help you improve, and by your second or third seam you'll be stitching curves at an astounding speed without even pinning.

The block is easiest to make in two contrasting colors. For your first attempt, I recommend fabrics with *low* contrast or small prints like positive-negative prints. Positive-negative prints are characterized by light print on a dark background and a matching print that is a dark print on a light background. *High*-contrast solid colors like red and white or blue and white are a traditional choice but can be difficult to successfully piece. The seams in this block are pressed toward the concave curve. On two of the seams the dark colored

seam will be under the light-colored piece. There is always the chance that the seam allowance of the darker fabric will shadow through a lighter fabric in the finished quilt. Solid fabrics, especially when combined with pastels or whites, will require extra

PIECING LESSON
Four Keys to Successfully Piecing Curves:

Pieced curves have the undeserved reputation of being difficult. In reality they are not hard to stitch accurately and in most cases don't even need to be pinned. Here is a list of hints to make sewing curves easier and help solve common problems.

▼ Stitch an accurate ¼" seam allowance. For a more accurate seam, determine the seam allowance from the pattern piece. To ensure the seams match the pattern, place the pattern piece under the needle and presser foot. Line up the needle with the seamline or matching points; then mark the seam allowance width on the needle plate. Mis-stitched seam allowances are one of the biggest problems in stitching curves. A lesson in basic geometry can explain what can go wrong. For a simple demonstration I'll use a two-piece block called *Drunkard's Path*. When the two halves of the block pattern lie together, it is easy to see the seamlines are a perfect match. Stitched with a perfect ¼" seam allowance, these two pieces make a square block. Stitched with less than a ¼" seam allowance, the length of the curved seams on the half blocks changes size. The concave seam becomes shorter, while the convex seam longer. When the two halves of the block lie together, the seamlines don't fit together. The pieces require easing or stretching to make the seamlines of equal length, and the block does not finish a true square. A similar, but opposite, effect occurs when the seam is stitched with a greater than ¼" seam allowance. The concave seam becomes longer, while the convex seam becomes shorter. Common problems that result from incorrect seam allowances are misshapen

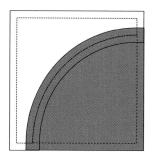

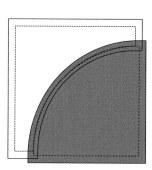

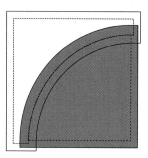

blocks, puckers or pleats along the curve seam, and seam wells.

▼ Use the right presser foot. To make a true ¼" seam you need a foot that gives a clear view of the fabric edges. I recommend a foot called a binder foot. This foot is available as an extra accessory for some brands of machines, or you can make a binder foot by altering a zigzag foot. The binder foot is a regular zig-zag foot that is missing the bridge (like the no bridge embroidery foot) and it's missing the entire right toe. It looks odd but works wonderfully. It gives a clear view of the seam allowance

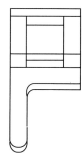

and the seamline right at the spot the needle is stitching. Feet that have a right hand toe conceal the seam. Because the two halves of the block curve in opposite directions, the seam allowances want to curve away from each other. Lining up seams as they go under the toe of a regular foot doesn't ensure a correctly stitched seam. Frequently when the seams line up at the toe of the foot, they are mis-matched at the needle. Binder foot allows a clear view of the stitching and gives you space to correct any problems. It is easy to use a pin point, seam ripper point, or even a hemostat to coax the seam allowances into the correct position right at the point the needle is forming the seam. To make a binder foot, use metal working tools to cut or grind away the bridge on the right hand toe of a regular zigzag foot. Then use a file to smooth the rough edges on the foot sole to insure the fabric feeds smoothly.

▼ Use as few pins as possible. Pinning on complex curves like *Candy Swirl* is often counterproductive. Pins don't hold the seam together accurately. The pins can slip and allow the fabric to shift. They also restrict your control on the stitching and fabric.

▼ To illustrate sewing an unpinned curve seam, I will use the *Drunkard's Path*. The same basic steps apply to all curved seams. I suggest you make your own practice sample as you follow my directions. For practicing curved seams, consider marking the matching dots on the right side of the convex curve and the wrong side of the concave curve as I did in the illustrations. This gives a clear view of all the dots and makes it easier to learn to match curves without pinning. For this sample, I made a series of clips along the seam allowance in the concave curve. The clips are about ⅛" deep and are ³⁄₁₆" to ¼" apart. On long or tight curves the clips are extremely important to insure a smooth seam. On short gentle curves, like this *Drunkard's Path*, the clips aren't necessary (although they make explaining and learning to stitch curved seams easier).

Begin by lining up the starting edges of the two pieces. Place the concave curve on the top, the convex on the bottom. Line up the outer edges that make the straight edge of the block. Allow the pieces to lie flat. The seam allowances do not line up around the entire curved seam. That is correct. Note that for a short distance at the beginning of the seam the seam allowances line up. Sew from the edge of the block that short distance, until the seam allowances start to curve away from each other. Here is where the binder foot is indispensable. The foot gives you a clear view of the seam allowances curving away from each other.

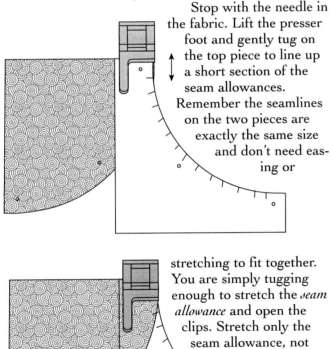

Stop with the needle in the fabric. Lift the presser foot and gently tug on the top piece to line up a short section of the seam allowances. Remember the seamlines on the two pieces are exactly the same size and don't need easing or stretching to fit together. You are simply tugging enough to stretch the *seam allowance* and open the clips. Stretch only the seam allowance, not the seamline. Work close to the presser foot.

Stretch only the section of curve you are stitching. When you stitch your first block, use the matching dots as a guide to judge the amount of stretching needed to make the perfect curve.

Use caution when stretching the concave curve. On a curve there are two different grain lines. Usually the beginning and end of the curve are on the straight of grain. These sections of the curve are stable and don't have much

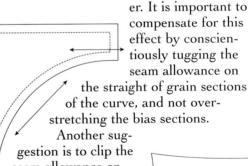

stretch. The center of the curve is usually on the bias. This section is very stretchy. There is a temptation to ignore stretching the straight of grain sections of the curve and to do all the stretching on the bias section. It is easy to sew this way, but can cause problems with the finished block. The most common result is that the finished block isn't square. When fabric stretches on the bias, the warp and weft threads shift. If you stretch a 2" bias strip, it will become narrower. The same thing is happening to the block. The sections that have been stretched change shape. If the bias is overstretched, the block will look like the illustration. The unstretched sections are the full width while the bias sections have become narrower. It is important to compensate for this effect by conscientiously tugging the seam allowance on the straight of grain sections of the curve, and not overstretching the bias sections.

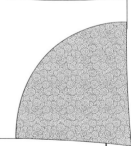

Another suggestion is to clip the seam allowance on the straight of grain sections and not the bias portions.

Work around the entire curved seam in short lines of stitching. Stitch the short section of seam where the seam allowances line up; then lift the presser foot line up a new section of seam, and stitch again. With practice you can combine these steps to make a smooth, unbroken line of stitching with a minimum of stopping, starting or lifting of the presser foot.

care and trimming to eradicate any possibility of fabric shadows.

BLOCK SIZE

9″

Pieces and corresponding strip sizes

Piece A: 11″ strips, the full width (42") of the fabric— yields 10 pieces

STRAIGHT SET PIECING DIRECTIONS

1. Cut the number of strips needed for the quilt size of your choice (see the chart, *Candy Swirl* Information (Straight Set), at the end of this section). Cutting strips of fabric makes it easier to both mark and cut the pieces.

2. Make a clear plastic template of piece A. Mark the dotted seamline on the template. Use a 1/16" punch to mark the matching dots on the template.

3. Trace the template onto the wrong side of the fabric as shown in the illustration at the top of the next column.

CUTTING HINT

Cutting Multiple Pieces: To save time and effort, mark and cut more than one layer of fabric at a time. Stack three or four single layers of fabric together, right side down. After stacking the layers, mark the pattern on the top layer and pin the layers together. Then cut the stack as a single piece. This method is fast but inaccurate if the layers shift during cutting. To prevent the fabrics from dislocating during cutting, use spray starch as a temporary "glue." To "glue" the fabric layers together, use the extra-heavy steam setting on a steam iron, or mist the fabric, to reactivate the existing starch you added to the fabrics. The starch will help keep the layers from separating and make the fabrics easier to cut.

The four pieces needed for each block can be layered and cut together. Simply layer the four fabric strips needed for each block, two lights and two darks, and cut. This method cuts an entire block at a time. The pieces can be cut with scissors or a rotary cutter. Scissors are best for the novice quilter. I suggest the rotary cutter for the proficient quilter who is adept and accurate with the rotary cutter. You could even have a Plexiglas template made of pattern piece A to make your rotary cutting easier.

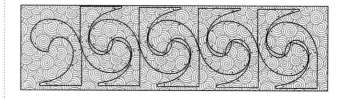

ROTARY CUTTING HINT

Precision Curves: A turn-table under the rotary mat and the smaller rotary cutter make it easier to cut accurate curves.

---

4. Before piecing, mark the matching dots on the four pieces of at least one block. The matching dots are not important after you learn how to piece the curve (I never use them on my own piecing). For the beginner, the dots help you learn the "feel" of stitching a curve.

5. Before you start to stitch, make a series of clips along the seam allowance in the concave curve. The clips are about 1/8" deep and are 3/16" to 1/4" apart. Stitch one dark piece A and one light piece A together. Line them up as illustrated, convex on the bottom, concave on the top. In the illustration, the light piece is on top of the dark, but it doesn't matter which color is on the top or bottom. Just make sure you are using two different colors with right sides together. Start stitching where the two pieces meet in the center of the block. Stitch the curve. The pattern is designed to facilitate the correct placement of the two pieces at the block edge. The concave curve is trimmed to match the block edge of the convex curve. Stitch along the curve until the curve begins to straighten, approximately 4" from the end of the seam. Line up the top and bottom pieces of the curve and pin the block edges together. Sew a 1/4" seam until you reach the end of the curve. Then angle towards the block edge, stitching diagonally to the point of the upper piece. You should be

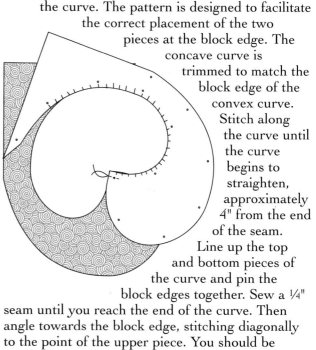

sewing off the point as you reach the block edge. Press the seams towards the concave curve. Press carefully without steam. Do not stretch the unstitched curves.

6. Complete the two half blocks. Lay the two halves together to form the complete block. There appears to be a single seam that joins the two halves, but it is impossible to accurately sew these tight curves in one line of stitching. Treat the seam as two seams, so the concave curve will always be on top of the convex when stitching the curve. Place one

half block on top of the other half block. Key the seams for an accurate match. Start stitching in the center of the block. Do not backstitch or knot the stitching line in the block center. Stitch the curved seam as the previous seams. Turn the block over and stitch the last seam of the block. Start stitching in the center. Overlap the beginning of the previous seam to secure the block center.

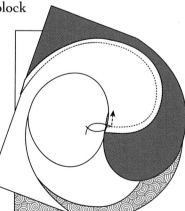

PIECING HINT

Straightening a Block: Did all the blocks turn out perfectly square? Perhaps some blocks look like the illustration. This effect is common when blocks contain curved seams. For a complete explanation of what went wrong see the piecing hint for curved seams, but for now don't throw away the less-than-perfect blocks. In most cases they are usable and no one will know your mistakes. The secret is knowing the correct location of the seamline and ¼" seam allowance. The outer edge is being pulled inward by the bias seam. That means the block is too small where the block edge curves. The simplest way to fix the slight discrepancy is to ignore the dip and sew "as if" there were a full ¼" seam allowance. This will work only if the dip is very shallow, under ⅛". If you got a very pronounced curve or dip when you pressed the block, you can try to correct the block by re-pressing and shaping it closer to the square shape. Use a blocking guide to help reshape the block. Draw a full size block, including the seam allowances, onto a piece of plain muslin. Place the drawing on the ironing board and place the pieced block over the guide. Use a combination of pinning and pressing to make the pieced block fit the guide. Plenty of steam and gentle easing or stretching will repair all but the worst blocks. If your attempts at straightening a badly misshapen block fail, I suggest you regard the block as a sample of what *not* to do, and throw it away.

Press the seams toward the concave curve. There is a problem in the block center where the seams meet. The seam allowances prevent pressing the seams in opposite directions. To solve the dilemma I use a great tip from Georgia Bonesteel. Look closely at the wrong side of the block center. The

PIECING HINT

Ripping Out Incorrect Stitching: I strongly believe there are only two forms of quiltmaking: Sewing and Throwing or Stitching and Pitching. Ripping doesn't fit the rhyme and it isn't my idea of fun. Ripping is a last resort I use only when forced to by a limited amount of fabric, or when I make a mistake toward the end of a complex block or quilt top. In most cases ripping distorts the pieces and weakens the seamline. If you must rip, use a sharp seam ripper and clip every third or four stitch on the bobbin side of the seam. A sharp tug on the top thread will undo the seam with the least amount of damage. Carefully re-press the piece to its correct size before trying to use it again.

The best suggestion I can make for ripping is to make a mutual agreement with a quilting friend: you rip for her; she rips for you. Surprisingly, ripping isn't a chore when you're not emotionally involved with the project. I suspect the real difficulty with ripping is psychological. When I need to rip I am not in a good frame of mind to do the ripping. I'm mad at myself for making the mistake and frequently make more of a muddle ripping than I had at the outset. When I learned to sew, my mother did all the ripping for me, and now we still rip for each other. I strongly suspect that's why I love to sew today. She knew how great it is to have someone else fix the mistake and return the pieces fresh and ready to sew.

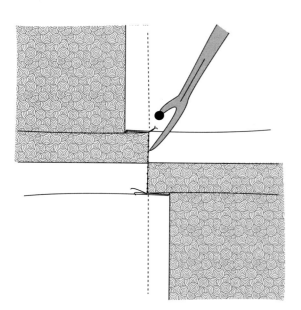

8. Join rows to complete the quilt body.

last seams sewn cross the two previous seams. Using a seam ripper, open the short section of the previous seams. Rip from the edge of the fabric to the seamline. With the stitching removed, the seam allowances are separated and the seams can be pressed to the correct side.

7. For the straight set, join the blocks into rows. The seams along the block edges will require careful matching. I suggest marking the matching dot on the seam along the block edge to help successfully match these unusual seams. Use the pattern template to mark the dots on the completed block. When you have completed joining the blocks, press the seams open. Refer to the Block Set in the chart, *Candy Swirl* Information (Straight Set), for the row arrangement needed for the quilt size of your choice.

9. Cut the borders from the required yardage. Cut four strips 8" wide by the required length. The four border strips will be the measure of the longest side plus 1". The borders can have butted or mitered corners.

10. Mark the quilting design on the borders. Choose a border pattern from the quilt pattern selection located in the back of the book.

11. The quilting pattern for the body of the quilt is a mini-clam shell. The curved shape

of the shells complements the curved piecing. Use invisible thread or fine neutral-colored thread to quilt the clamshell.

12. Stitch the backing together and prepare the quilt for quilting. Layer and baste the quilt.

13. Quilt the quilt and finish with ½" wide French bias binding.

DIAGONAL SET PIECING DIRECTIONS

Refer to Block Set in the chart, *Candy Swirl* Information (Diagonal Set), for the number of blocks and the row arrangement needed for the quilt size of your choice. Piece the diagonal set exactly like the straight set, with the exception of the partial blocks required on the edge of the quilt body.

This is an extraordinary pattern because of the construction of the half blocks used on the quilt edge. To give credit to the old saying, "every rule is meant to be broken," the half blocks in this quilt are truly "half" blocks. You cut one completed block in half to make two triangle-shaped blocks for the quilt edge! Cutting a block in half to form two usable blocks is extremely unusual and often considered incorrect. In this pattern the half block simplifies the pattern. The half block prevents the formation of a small crescent-shaped piece in the block center that occurs if you cut the block in the traditional way used in *Stars and Bars*. Compare the two illustrations. Note the crescent shape in the first one detracts from the quilt. It looks confusing, as if you miscut the half blocks. With the block cut exactly in half, the quilt edges are simpler and neater. Not only does the half block remove the crescent shape, it also removes the points of the full blocks around the quilt edges.

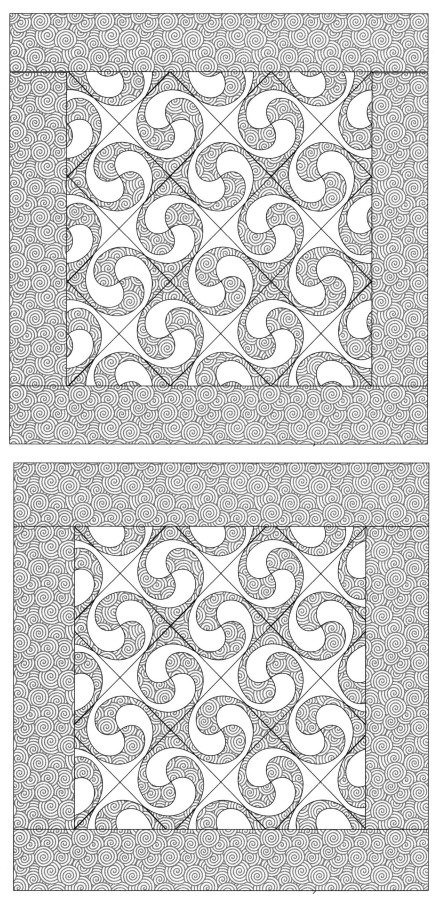

Candy Swirl Information (Straight Set)

	Crib	Twin	Double	Queen	King
Finished size	43 × 52	70 × 97	79 × 107	88 × 107	115 × 115
Border width	8"	8"	8"	8"	8"
Block set	3 x 4	6 x 9	7 x 10	8 x 10	11 x 11
Total blocks	12	54	70	80	121
Amount of fabric required (in yards)					
Two colors (each color)	1	3½	4⅜	5	7¾
Borders with mitered corners	1⅝	2¾	3⅛	3⅛	3¼
Backing	1⅝	5½	6¼	9¼	9⅞
Bias binding	½	⅞	⅞	1	1⅛
Cutting Guide					
Blocks, 11" strips (each color)	3	10	14	16	25
Total piece A (each color)	24	108	140	160	242

Candy Swirl Information (Diagonal Set)

	Crib	Twin	Double	Queen	King
Finished size	41 × 68	68 × 92	80 × 92	92 × 105	118 × 118
Border width	8"	8"	8"	8"	8"
Block set	2 × 4	4 × 6	5 × 6	6 × 7	8 × 8
Total blocks, including those used for half and quarter blocks	16	48	60	84	128
Total blocks cut in half to make two half blocks	4	8	9	11	14
Amount of fabric required (in yards)					
Two colors (each color)	1⅜	3¼	3¾	5⅜	8
Borders with mitered corners	2	2¾	2¾	3	3⅜
Backing	2	5¼	5¼	9	10
Bias binding	⅝	⅞	⅞	1	1⅛
Cutting Guide					
Blocks, 11" strips (each color)	4	10	12	17	26
Total piece A (each color)	32	96	120	168	256

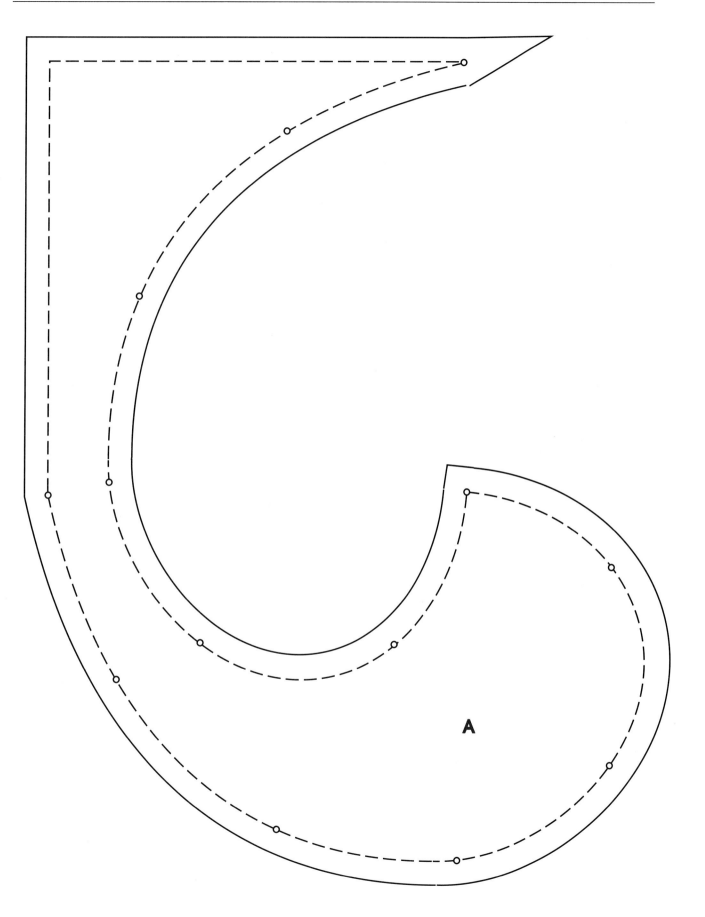

A

Chapter 4

DIAMONDS

Hexagon Stars

Hexagon Stars is a wonderful introduction to diamond patterns. Like many overall patterns, hexagon stars can have many layers of design. The obvious design is the six-pointed star in the center of a hexagon. A closer look reveals another six pointed star formed by the triangles. Conscientious use of color and contrast can give a quilt remarkable three-dimensional effects. The design offers a complex range of possiblities, but the pattern is simple. This pattern uses two main pieces, a 60-degree diamond and a triangle. Both pieces are perfect for rotary cutting. The stitching is straightforward enough for a novice quilt maker. The pattern is based on hexagons, but the addition of triangles makes the quilt a straight set. I've also included an alternative edge finish to make the quilt edges straight. *Hexagon Stars* is one of those great patterns that looks difficult, but is a breeze to make.

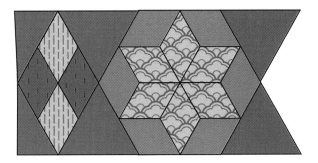

Block size

Hexagon is 10" high and 12" wide

Pieces and corresponding strip sizes

Piece A (diamonds): 3" strip, the full width—yields 11 pieces

Piece B (large triangle): 5¾" strip, the full width—yields 11 pieces

Piece C (half of triangle C to form a straight edge): 6⅛" strip, the full width—yields 22 pieces

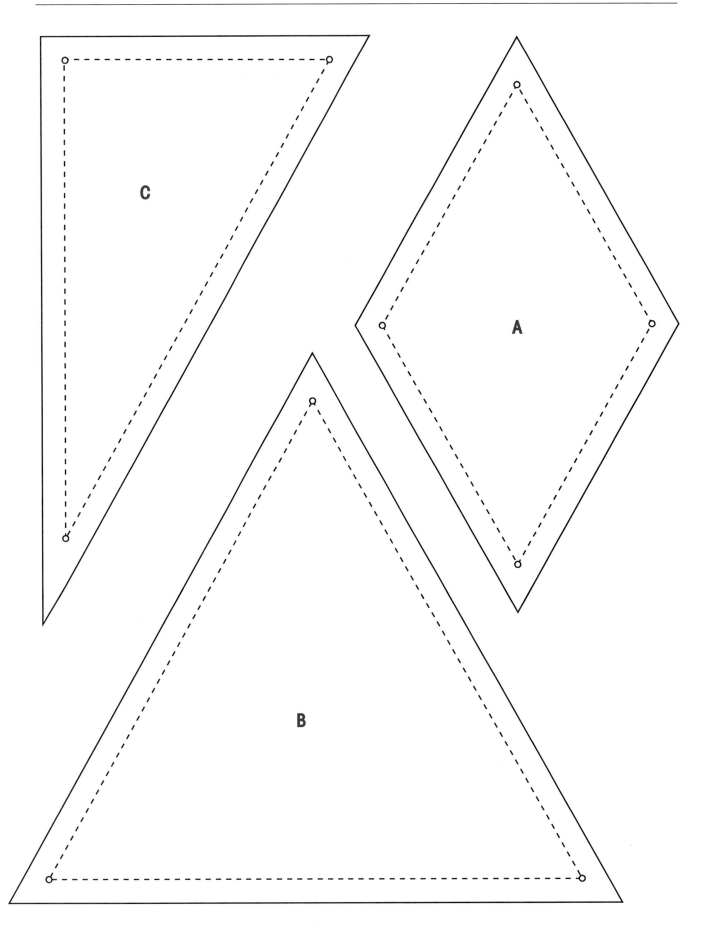

PIECING DIRECTIONS

1. Cut the number of strips required for the quilt size of your choice. See chart, *Hexagon Stars* Information, at the end of this section.

2. Make a paper or plastic template of diamond A. Tape it to the straight edge of a 6" × 12" ruler. Using the A strips, stack two to four strips for cutting multiple pieces. Cut the required number of diamonds in the star and field colors. The star color is the color or print that make the six pointed star. The field color is the color or print that surrounds the six pointed star.

3. Make a paper or plastic template of triangle B. Tape it to a 60-degree triangle. Using the B strips, stack two to four strips for cutting multiple pieces. Cut the required number of triangles.

4. Make a paper or plastic template of triangle C. Use a 90/60-degree triangle rather than the more common 90/45 degree triangle to rotary-cut this piece. Or make your own plastic template using a rotary template making kit.

MARKING HINT

Matching Dots on Multiple Cut Pieces: Every seam in the hexagon star is an inset seam. To inset a piece requires that the seam stop or start ¼" from the fabric edge. The inset seams must be accurate to insure the block fits together and finishes the correct size. Usually the stops and starts for a seam are marked with matching dots. The matching dots are lacking when these pieces are multiple cut with either a scissors or rotary cutter. You can use a plastic template and mark every dot on each individual piece. Or you could use a ruler and measure and mark a ¼" seam allowance around every piece. Matching dots are essential to the beginner. Matching dots helps line up every seam and join on the block.

But I am the first to agree that marking every dot or seam line on every piece is a terrible job. It's boring and slow. There are alternatives for the accomplished quilter. I frequently use two methods. One is mass marking; the other uses seam guides. Mass marking and seam guides are fast effective ways to locate the matching dots on rotary cut pieces. The methods work well with any shaped piece including, diamond and hexagon shaped pieces.

MARKING HINT

Mass Marking Matching Dots: Mass marking is an effective way to mark many layers of blocks with the least amount of effort. It is my method of choice when working with small projects that involve multiple insets or difficult matches. The pieces are stacked in a group and the matching dots are marked with a pin. The pin acts as a skewer through all the fabric layers. The dots are then hand-marked at the spot the pin pierces the fabric.

To do a mass marking, stack the pieces together right sides up on a soft surface like an ironing board. Perfectly align the edges and corners of the pieces as they are stacked. The stack of fabrics can be ½" to ¾" thick. Depending on your fabric, that is about 30 to 50 pieces. Using a paper or plastic template of the pieces, place the template on top of the stack of pieces. With long, straight quilting pins skewer the stack of pieces, using one pin for every matching dot. Drive the pins straight through the stack, and the points into the ironing board. Pick up the stack with the pins still in the fabric. Pull the stack and pins completely off the ironing board. Turn the stack over to expose the pin points. Do not remove the pins. Work from the wrong side of the stack, pin points up. Use a fabric marker to mark a dot at the spot the pin pierces the fabric. Place the mark as close as possible to the pin and be neat. Mark the first piece and slip the piece off the stack and pins, then mark each successive piece until you have completed the stack. This is a great job to do while watching TV.

MARKING HINT

Using Seam Allowances to Locate Matching Dots: This is my personal favorite for large, simple inset seams like the Hexagon Star. It's fast, painless and doesn't require any fabric markers. This method uses layers of tape as a seam guide. The pieces are butted against the guide and ensure a perfect start every time.

Every quilter is familiar with seam guides used to mark the ¼" seam. They are metal guides or layers of tape that form a ridge on the needle plate to the right side of the presser foot. The fabric is held against the guide as it is sewn, ensuring a perfect ¼". Seam guides are not consigned to the right hand side of the presser foot or to the needle plate. Seam guides can be placed anywhere on the flat bed surface of the machine. First make a tape seam guide. Use electrician's tape or vinyl tape. These tapes are kinder to the finish of your machine than masking tape. (No matter what type of tape you use, remove it from the machine every night and clean your machine with WD40 to remove the tape residue.) Layer three pieces of tape about 3" long. Stack them one on top of the other, lining up the straight edges. Set this aside for now. Use the cutting template to correctly place the seam guide. It is always a good idea to begin stitching on the edge that has the inset seam. Place the template under the pressure foot as illustrated. Line up the template so the matching dot is directly under the needle. Lower the needle through the template. Hold the template as if you were sewing the seam. Place the tape seam guide along the starting edge of the template. For this pattern the seam guide is to the left and back of the presser foot. Remove the template from the machine and you're ready to try out this method. Place two A pieces right sides together. Align the edges. Place the pieces under the raised presser foot. Butt the starting edge against the shallow raise of the seam guide. Line up the right edge of the piece with the ¼" mark, and lower the presser foot. Don't worry about the seam guide affecting the feed of the fabric. Simply lift the starting edge of the fabric to clear the guide after you've made the knot and started to sew. The guide will not interfere with the seam. That's it! You're ready to sew.

5. Join the diamonds to make the star. Start on the inset side of the seam. Make a secure knot at the matching dot. Stitch across the pieces and off the edge of the fabric at the 60-degree point. Do not end the seam ¼" in from the edge as you did at the seam start.

Stitch the stars together. Stitch the diamonds in sets of three. Press open all seams as they are stitched. Join the two sets of three to make the star. Use a stab pin to ensure a perfect match in the star center. Start the center seam as with all previous seams, using the matching dots or seam guide. Stitch towards the center. This seam is unique because it both begins and ends with an inset seam. Both ends must be knotted ¼" from the fabric edge. If you

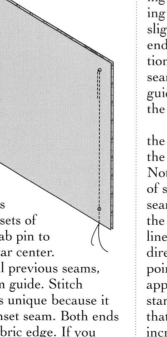

used the mass-marking method to mark the matching dots you will simply sew matching dot to matching dot and knot. But the seam guide method has a slight problem. Beginning the seam is easy, but the end of the seam is unmarked. There is an easy solution. Make another tape seam guide for ending this seam. Repeat the steps used to position the first guide. This guide will be in front and to the left of the foot.

Another trick to making a good match is to use the short section of seam, apparent in the seam allowance, as a stitching guide. Notice the short portion of stitching on the seam allowance of the last seam. That line of stitching leads directly to the center point of the star. As you approach the center of the star, stitch in the ditch along that seam line and you will increase your accuracy in matching the star center.

MATCHING HINT

Flag Matching Star Centers: Like other flag matches, the seam and seam allowance flags in the center of a six pointed star can be used to simplify matching points. The seams offer two clues to successfully matching the star center. One clue is the small triangle-shaped flag of seam allowance that extends beyond the edge of the center seam of the star. That triangle is the result of pressing open the seams. It always falls in the exact center of the star. To make a match, place the flag on the upper half of the star directly on top of the flag on the lower half of the star. When flag triangles line up the seams match.

Depending on your level of accuracy, you can use the triangles to determine the match and completely omit pinning. I often use this fast piecing trick with practical quilts I make for use, not as heirlooms.

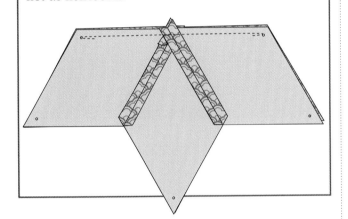

6. Inset the six diamonds around the star. Sew with the single diamond on the bottom and the star pieces on top. Sew from the edge of the pieces, toward the inset match.

Sew off the edge of the pieces at the other end of the seam. Only the seams at the 120-degree inset corners require starting and stopping at the matching dot. Press open the seams.

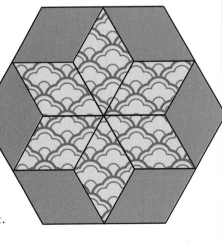

PIECING HINT

Pinless Insets: Surprisingly, insets are easy to do and match up, even easier than the star center! Begin by placing the field diamond under the star. Always sew with the star on the top, the single diamond on the bottom. Line up the single diamond and the star diamond so all the edges match. The key to a successful inset is lining up the corner of the lower piece to the inset seam. Don't waste time with matching dots or pins. The key to the match is in the seam allowances of the star. Of course, the outside edges of the lower diamond should match the outside edges of the diamond in the star. But the diamonds must match on all four sides, including the edges that are part of seams. To correctly line up the diamonds, tip back the inset seam as illustrated. Now line up the lower diamond so the edge of the lower diamond is lined up with the edge of the pressed-open seam allowance. Look closely at the illustration.

Notice the diamond edge is matching the seam allowance edge. Return the upper diamond to the original location and proceed with a standard inset seam.

7. Construct the half blocks required to make a straight-edge quilt. The blocks are made of four diamonds—two star color, two field color. Use the "needle down start" to join the diamonds. Note none of the seams are inset seams. Sew from edge to edge in every seam.

To begin the half block, join two diamonds—one star color, one field color—to make a diamond unit. Press open the seam. Repeat to make another diamond unit.

8. To complete the block, join the units of two to make the larger four-pieced diamond. Place the diamond units so the field color diamonds make the upper and lower diamond in the half block. Use the seam allowance flags to match the center seam. To make a match, place the flag on the upper diamond unit directly on top of the flag on the lower diamond unit. When flag triangles line up, the seams match. Refer to the chart, *Hexagon Stars* Information, for the number of half blocks required for the quilt size of your choice.

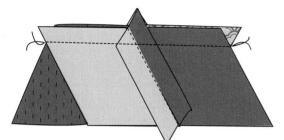

9. Join the triangles B and C to the hexagons to make the straight rows. Refer to the Block Set in the chart, *Hexagon Set* Information for the number of blocks and the row arrangement needed for the quilt size of your choice. The first row in *every* set is the row that starts with a half block. The next row contains all full blocks. When the Block Set states the quilt is 3 × 5, it means the first row is made of a half block, two full blocks, and a half block. The second row is 3 full blocks. The odd rows are identical. All the even rows are identical.

10. Join the rows to make the quilt. Use the stab pins for the matches, or use the triangle flag technique.

11. The quilting pattern I chose for this quilt is *Hanging Diamonds*. It is an overall pattern based on the 60-degree angle of the blocks. The pattern doesn't have to be marked on the quilt top. The piecing can serve as a guide. If you prefer, you can mark the top. The lines are 1¼" apart. I recommend using a walking foot and invisible thread or fine neutral-colored thread to quilt the grid. For more information on grid quilting, see the chapter, Machine Quilting Update.

12. Stitch the backing together and prepare the quilt for quilting. Layer and baste the quilt.

13. Quilt the quilt and finish with ½"-wide French bias binding.

Hexagon Stars Information

	Crib	Twin	Double	Queen	King
Finished size	35" × 50"	80" × 90"	80" × 100"	103" × 100"	115" × 110"
Block set	3 × 5	7 × 9	7 × 10	9 × 10	10 × 11
Total full blocks	12	58	65	85	104
Total partial blocks	6	10	10	10	12
Amount of fabric required (in yards)					
Stars, one color	¾	3	3¼	4⅛	5
Hexagon field	¾	3	3¼	4⅛	5
Triangles	¾	2	2⅜	3⅛	3½
Backing	1½	5¼	5¾	8½	9½
Bias binding for straight edge quilt	½	⅞	⅞	1	1⅛
Cutting Guide					
Blocks					
Star color, piece A, 3" strips	8	34	38	49	59
Field color, piece A, 3" strips	8	34	38	49	59
Total piece A (each color)	84	368	410	530	648
Triangle B, 5¾" strips	3	11	12	16	19
Total piece B	24	116	130	170	208
Triangle C, 6⅛" strips	1	2	2	2	2
Total piece C	20	36	40	40	44

Chapter 5
HEXAGONS

Introduction to Hexagon-Based Patterns

Hexagons are one of the most diverse of pieced patterns. Combined with the companion pieces, squares, 60-degree diamonds, and triangles, hexagons can produce thousands of different pattern variations. Many of the patterns are familiar, such as *Baby Blocks, Hexagon Star,* and *Grandmother's Flower Garden.* These traditional patterns are the most sedate of the design possibilities. More exciting designs include *Ozark Tile, Columbian Star,* and *Nine-Patch Star.* The array of design possibilities is overwhelming. They run the gamut from ultra-conservative to completely contemporary. The basic shapes can be cut, twisted, and fitted together to form larger and more complex hexagon shapes.

There are several ways to work with hexagon-based designs by machine. In the tradtional way, the hexagons are cut and sewn as hexagons. This means inset seams and change in the way we perceive machine piecing. The methods are not hard, but more time-intensive. With the advent of rotary cutters, many patterns are frequently simplified to make the seams all straight edges. Hexagons are easily cut in half or into equilateral triangles. These shapes are simpler to cut and sew than the hexagon block. This idea is wonderful, I advocate it, and even use it in this book. But I know that split hexagons have their limitations. For one, cutting the hexagon requires a large-scale design. Cutting small hexagons results in even smaller pieces with many more seams and matches. Splitting the hexagons can also limit or compromise the design. It is a trade-off: there are new designs possible by splitting the hexagons, but there are some losses. For me, the last reason against split hexagons is more personal than professional. Cutting the block to make it easier to sew reduces an intrinsic element of the design. Part of the lure of the hexagon patterns is the skill they require to construct. To me, hexagons are a statement about my quilting expertise.

The following chapters show many ways of dealing with hexagon designs, some traditional, some contemporary. They combine the best of both worlds and make hexagon-based designs challenging, interesting, and fun. The key to working successfully with hexagons is knowing the basic piecing methods and how to apply them to the different variations. There are two basic piecing methods: row and motif.

The methods all use the inset seam to construct the designs, but the order in which the pieces are put together is based on a logical sequence determined by the type of pattern. For example, the row method is used for patterns like *Tumbling Blocks* and *Church Windows*. In these patterns the pieces appear to be stacked in rows. By comparison the motif method is used for designs like *Grandmother's Flower Garden* or *Hexagon Stars*. In these patterns the pieces make a motif.

Using these basic methods makes machine stitching hexagons logical and easy. Surprisingly, the majority of pieces are simple to rotary-cut and the matches are intermediate inset piecing. To present the information logically, the designs will be presented by method of construction: first row, then interlocking motif, and finally, large motifs. Each chapter builds on the previous information and offers patterns to showcase your new skills.

Row-Based Hexagon Designs

Basic Piecing Method

As the name implies, row-based designs are constructed in rows of blocks, much like brick laying. There are no long zig-zag seams joining the rows of hexagons. In this method the hexagons are added one at a time to the previous rows. Row based designs are the simplest to sew. The method works extremely well with large, multi-pieced hexagon blocks like the *Diamond Nine Patch*. It is also the method of choice for small complex piecing like *Quintettes* and *Ozark Tile*. The most common row based hexagon design is *Tumbling Blocks*.

The basic instructions use a simple hexagon block to explain the technique. I suggest you make this 20 block sample to try out the row construction. The row layout is five blocks wide by four rows high.

Row Construction

The sample requires ¼ yard of scrap fabrics. Cut two strips 3" wide. From those strips cut 18 hexagons. Cut the hexagon pieces with scissors or rotary cutter. Either way, it is necessary to mark all the dots on every piece. All seams in hexagon designs are inset seams. These seams start and stop ¼" from the edge of the fabric. This requires matching dots to indicate the exact spot to start and stop sewing.

Row One

1. Lay out the pattern pieces as shown. There are five rows of blocks.

PIECING HINT

Using a Binder Foot for Inset Piecing: I recommend a foot called a binder foot for inset piecing. This foot is a regular zig-zag foot that is missing the bridge (like the no-bridge embroidery foot) and it's missing the entire right toe. It looks odd but works wonderfully. It gives a clear view of the seam allowance and the seam line right at the spot the needle is stitching. Feet that have a right hand toe conceal the seam. The binder foot allows a clear view of the stitching and gives you space to correct any problems. It is easy to use a pin point, seam ripper point, or even a hemostat to coax the seam allowances into the correct position right at the point the needle is forming the seam. For more information, see Chapter 8, Quilter's Schoolhouse.

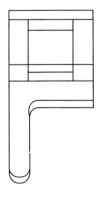

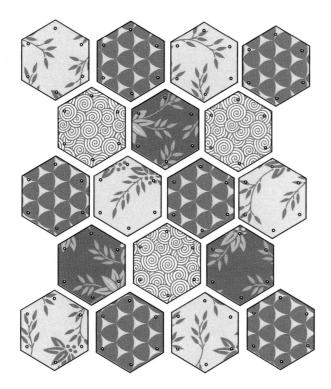

2. Start stitching with the bottom row. Join the four blocks across that row. Remember they are inset seams. The seam must start and stop at the matching dots. Press open all the seams.

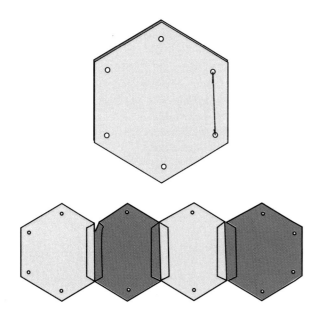

Row Two

3. In this method individual blocks are added to previous rows. You will not join completed rows to completed rows. The first block of the second row is stitched to the first row. It is an inset

seam and will be stitched on two sides. The illustration shows the two edges that will be stitched. The first row and the single hexagon are wrong side up on a table. It is a good idea to use pins to mark the edges that will be stitched first. Place a pin in the edge of the hexagon row and the matching edge of the single hexagon. Pin-marking the correct edges

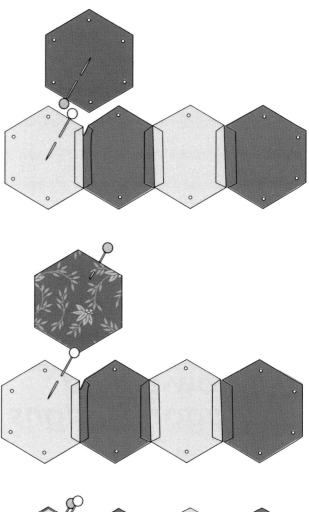

reduces the confusion in complex designs. Flip the single hexagon right side up as shown in the illustration. Slide the single hexagon right side up under the first hexagon in the first row. The two edges with the pins should be together. Line up the edges of the hexagons and pin the hexagon in place. The

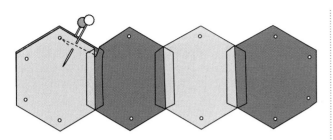

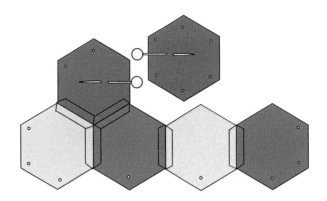

single hexagon is now on the bottom and the wrong side of the row is on top. The open seam of the inset is clearly visible.

Inset piecing is used in all seams of hexagon based designs. The insets for hexagons are easy; in fact, plain hexagons rarely require pinning. The trick to stitching hexagon insets is in lining up the hexagon pieces. The key to remember: Always place the lower hexagon directly under the upper hexagon. All the edges should match. For easiest placement use the seam allowance for a guide. For basic instructions, see the piecing hint, *Pinless Inset,* in the chapter, *Hexagon Stars*.

Start sewing at the matching dot, sewing toward the open seam. Stitch toward the open corner of the inset corner. Stitch across the open seam allowance. The last stitch before turning the corner should fall off the folded edge of the top fabric, as close as possible to the knot or backstitching in the open seam. Stop with the needle lowered in the single layer of fabric of the lower hexagon. Lift the presser foot, pivot the fabrics to turn the corner. Line up the seam allowances of the upper and lower hexagons. *Also,* make sure all the edges of the upper and lower hexagons match. Lower the presser foot and continue sewing. Remember, stop and start at marking dots. Press open the seams.

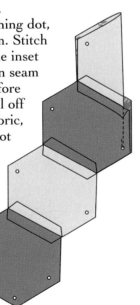

4. The next hexagon in the second row will be stitched on three sides. Place the body of the quilt (the quilt body is the first row and any pieces stitched to that row) wrong side up on the table. Place the single hexagon wrong side up as shown in the illustration. Place a marking pin in the two edges that will be stitched first. Then flip the single hexagon right side up and slide it under the first hexagon in the second row. Line up all the edges of

the hexagons and pin the hexagon in place. The single hexagon is now on the bottom and the wrong side of the quilt body is on the top. The open seams of the insets are clearly visible.

Start sewing at the matching dot, sewing toward the first open seam. Stitch toward the open seam of the inset corner. Stitch across the open seam allowance. The last stitch before turning the corner should fall off the folded edge of the top fabric, as close as possible to the knot or backstitching in the open seam. Stop with the needle lowered in the single layer of fabric in the lower hexagon. Lift the presser foot, and pivot the fabrics to turn the corner. Lower the presser foot and continue sewing toward the second open seam. Stitch the second inset as the first. Remember, stop and start at marking dots. Press open the seams.

5. Repeat step 4 across the row.

Row Three
6. To make the edges of the quilt balance, the first block of the third row and every odd row must extend one hexagon beyond the even rows. (Depending on how you start the quilt, on some quilts the even rows are longer than the odd rows. But no matter which way you start the quilt, the rows must alternate between extended rows and regular rows.) Notice that the first, third, and fifth row extend beyond the second and fourth rows. The first hexagon on the odd rows will be stitched on only one side of the hexagon. For the beginner, it is a good idea to use pins to mark the edges that will be stitched together. Place a pin in the first edge of the hexagon row and the matching edge of the single hexagon. It can be confusing to determine which edge is correct when the blocks are turned wrong side up. To start the odd rows, place the body of the quilt wrong side up on the table top. Place the single hexagon as shown in the illustration. Flip the

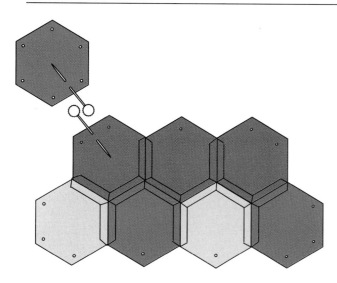

hexagon right side up and slide the single hexagon under the first hexagon in the second row. Line up the edges of the hexagons and pin the hexagon in place. The single hexagon is now on the bottom and the wrong side of the quilt body is on top. Remember this seam is also an inset. Stop and start at marking dots. Join the single hexagon and press open the seam.

7. The next hexagon in the third row will be stitched on three sides. Follow step 4. Repeat step 4 across the row. The last hexagon in the row will extend beyond the previous row. It will be stitched on only two sides.

Rows Four and Five

Follow the previous directions, alternating even and odd rows. Use directions for row 2 as a guide to stitching all the even rows. Use the directions for row 3 as a guide for all odd rows.

Colombian Star

The *Colombian Star* is the perfect introduction to hexagon-row patterns. The diamonds and hexagon blocks can be rotary-cut. The blocks are large and the matches are straightforward enough for a beginner. This combination of *Tumbling Blocks* and solid hexagons forms an overall pattern of stars floating on a hexagon field. The effect of the design depends on the color choice and placement. The Tumbling Blocks are made from three values—light, medium, and dark—and you could introduce another value in the solid hexagons. With the different values and large pieces, the quilt is perfect for using an assortment of print or plain scrap fabrics. Antiques made from this pattern frequently contained plaids and stripes. The effect is dizzying and delightful. The plain hexagon is most evident when it is made from either the lightest or darkest fabric and offers a large plain space for the quilted feathered wreath. The pattern is a natural for making a straight-edged quilt. With careful planning you can arrange the blocks so the solid hexagons make the partial blocks at the quilt edge. The solid block is easy to cut in half and it reduces the number of partial blocks that require piecing. The quilt is finished with a border and contrasting binding.

BLOCK SIZE

Straight edge to straight edge 8½"
Point to point 9¾"

Pieces and corresponding strip sizes
Piece A, solid hexagon: 9"strip—yields 4 pieces
Piece A1, half hexagon: 4¾" strip—yields 5 pieces
Piece B, diamond: 4¾" strip—yields 7 pieces

PIECING DIRECTIONS

1. Cut the number of strips required for the quilt size of your choice.

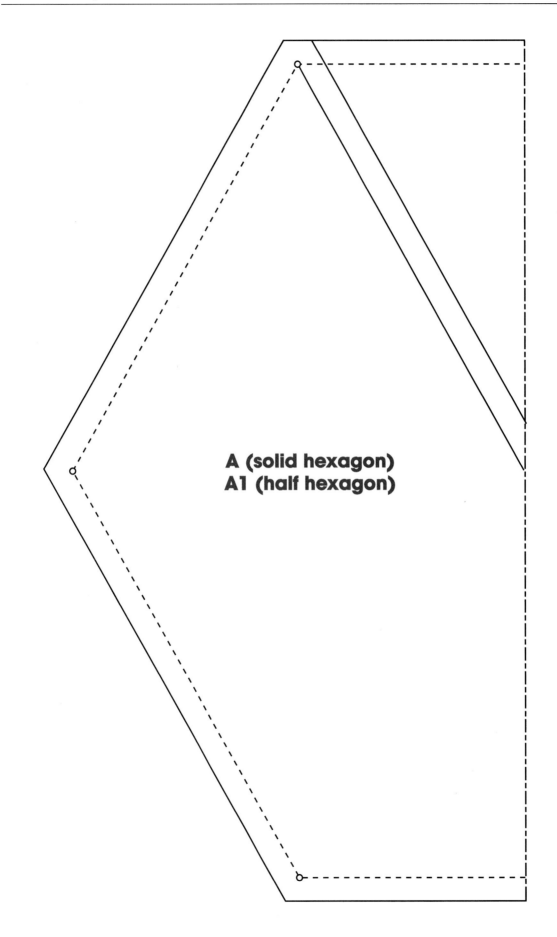

A (solid hexagon)
A1 (half hexagon)

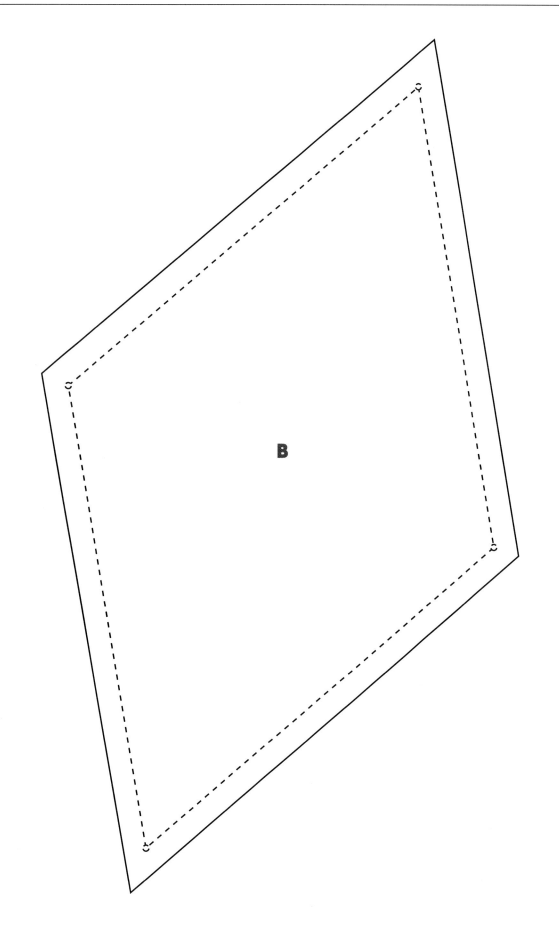

2. Make the three pattern templates. The large hexagon pattern is too large for the page. Two half patterns will make one large hexagon (see illustration). To make the half hexagon, use the large hexagon and cut it diagonally as illustrated. Use paper or plastic or you may choose to use heavy template plastic or Plexiglas for rotary templates. This pattern is suited to rotary cutting, but does not require special rotary templates.

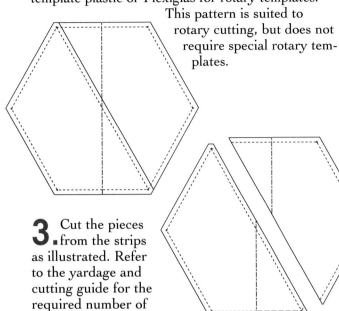

3. Cut the pieces from the strips as illustrated. Refer to the yardage and cutting guide for the required number of pieces in each color.

ROTARY CUTTING HINT

Rotary Cutting Large Pieces: The solid hexagon and half hexagons can be cut using a rotary cutter, but the large size pattern piece doesn't fit on most rulers or triangles. An easy way to work with such large pieces is to combine hand tracing and rotary cutting. Begin by layering the required strips. Hand trace around the template onto the top strip. *Note:* With careful tracing, the edges of the hexagons line up so two cuts with the rotary cutter will cut four sides of the hexagons. Use a standard-size ruler (12" × 6") to rotary cut along the lines.

4. Matching dots are required to sew this pattern. I recommend the mass marking method to locate the matching dots (see the marking hint, *Mass Marking Matching Dots* in the section, *Hexagon Stars*). Mass-mark all the matching dots on the solid and half hexagons and diamonds.

5. Begin by making the required number of complete Tumbling Blocks. Refer to the chart, *Colombian Star* Information, at the end of this section, for the requirments for the quilt size of your choice. Do not make the partial blocks at this time. All the Tumbling Blocks in the sample have identical color placement. This arrangement is the easiest to lay out and plan, but is not the only choice. You may choose to experiment with other sequences prior to stitching the blocks. For the sample all the blocks are constructed as illustrated.

6. To make a Tumbling Block, stitch the two diamonds together that bracket the inset. In the illustration this is the dark and medium diamonds. The seam must start exactly on the matching dot on the 120-degree angle (that's the wide angle). Make a secure knot and sew across the seam and off the edge of the pieces. Press open the seams.

7. Inset the light diamond into the two pieces. Sew with the light diamond on the bottom and the two pieces on top. Sew from the edge of the pieces toward the inset match.

Sew off the edge of the pieces at the other end of the seam. Press open the seams.

8. Lay out the first row of *Tumbling Blocks*. The first row (and all even rows) is always a row of Tumbling Blocks without solid hexagons. The illustration shows a simplified layout. Join all the blocks in this row following the basic instructions for row construction.

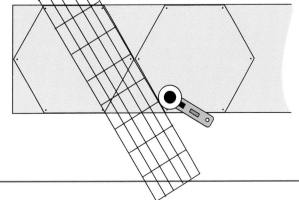

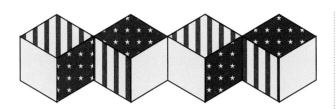

9. Lay out the second row of hexagons, half hexagons, and Tumbling Blocks. Alternate the Tumbling Blocks with solid hexagons. Start the second row with a half hexagon block (piece A1). Depending on the size of your quilt, the row may end with a half hexagon or partial Tumbling Block. If this row ends with a partial Tumbling Block as shown in the illustration, use only two diamonds to make this block. When making the partial Tumbling Block simply sew from edge to edge. This is not an inset seam.

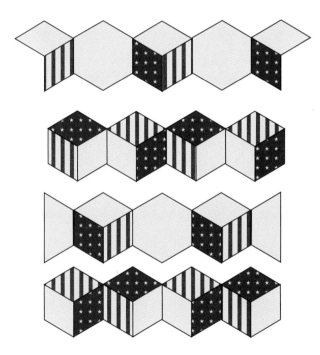

10. Join the blocks of the second row to the first row, following the basic instructions for row construction.

11. Lay out the remaining rows and join the pieces to the quilt body following the basic instructions.

12. Add a row of finishing diamonds to the top and bottom edges of the quilt body. Inset with row construction. These diamonds may not be required on both edges of the quilt, depending on the quilt size. The diamonds can be in any of the three colors. I used the light value. The diamonds will be used to make the straight edge on the quilt.

MARKING HINT

Matches for Tumbling Blocks: When joining the Tumbling Blocks to make a row, you need a matching dot to begin and end the seam. One dot is on the 120-degree angle. The other end of the seam falls in the seams from the Tumbling Blocks (see the illustration). This matching dot is hidden by the previous seam. I suggest beginners mark this matching dot along the inset seam of the Tumbling Blocks using the diamond pattern B. For advanced quilters, the seam line can be used in place of the matching dot.

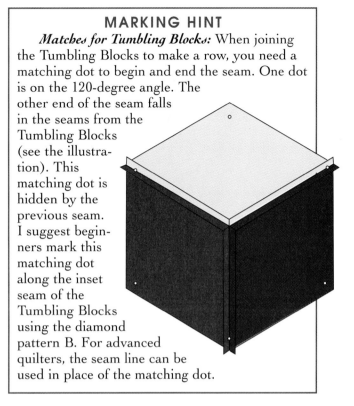

13. The partial blocks on the four quilt edges must be cut to make the quilt edge straight. Remember the cut edge is ¼" beyond the exact center of the block. For the top and bottom edge use a 24" ruler and place the ¼" mark of the ruler over the block centers. In this quilt the center falls through the points of the diamond. Use a fabric marker to mark along the ruler edge. For the sides of the quilt line up the ruler with the straight edges of the half hexagon and straight diamonds in the partial blocks. (To be on the safe side, I don't recommend novice quilters cut the blocks until after the border is stitched in place. The experienced quilter may choose to rotary-cut the quilt edge as it is measured.) Straighten the quilt as illustrated.

14. Cut the borders from the required yardage. Cut four strips 9" wide by the required length. The four border strips will be the measure of the longest side plus 1". The border can have butted or mitered corners.

15. Mark the quilting design on the border. Use a pattern from the selection in Chapter 7, Quilting Patterns for Borders.

16. The quilting design for the large hexagon is a feathered wreath. The quilting design for the star blocks is a continuous-curve design. Mark the designs on the quilt top.

17. Stitch the backing together and prepare the quilt for quilting. Layer and baste the quilt.

18. Quilt the quilt and finish with ½"-wide French bias binding.

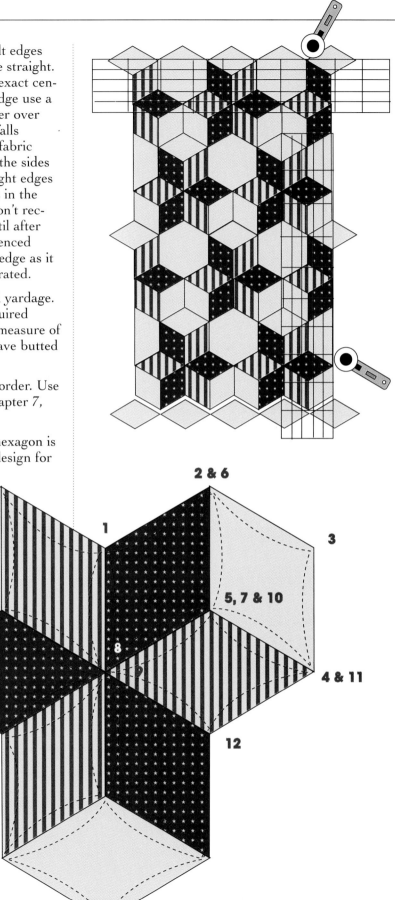

Colombian Star Information

	Crib	Twin	Double	Queen	King
Finished size	—	69" × 91"	78" × 91"	86" × 105"	103" × 113"
Border width	—	9"	9"	9"	9"
Block set	—	6 × 10	7 × 10	8 ×12	10 ×13
Number of blocks	—	60	70	96	130
Amount of fabric required (in yards)					
Solid hexagons, half hexagons, finishing diamonds	—	1¼	1⅔	2⅓	2⅝
Tumbling Blocks (each of three values)	—	1	1¼	1⅝	2
Borders with butted corners	—	2¾	2¾	3	3¼
Backing	—	2¾	5½	6	10
Bias binding	—	¾	⅞	1	1⅛
Cutting Guide					
Solid hexagons A, 9" strips	—	3	4	6	7
Total solid hexagons	—	12	15	21	27
Half hexagons A1, 4¾" strips	—	2	1	2	2
Total half hexagons	—	6	5	6	6
Tumbling Block diamonds, 4¾" strips (each of three values)	—	7	9	11	15
Total diamonds (each of three values)	—	47	62	75	103
Total complete Tumbling Blocks	—	43	57	69	97
Total partial Tumbling Blocks (do not make these blocks until needed)	—	4	5	6	6
Finishing diamonds, 4¾" strip	—	1	2	3	3
Total finishing diamonds	—	7	8	9	11

Nine Patch Diamond

The *Nine Patch Diamond* is a wonderful complex-looking pattern that has a single pattern piece. And that piece is entirely rotary-cut. Although the pattern appears difficult it is a really an intermediate pattern. The matches are not hard, but there are a lot of them. To make the quilt top easier to piece, the nine-patch diamonds are joined in sets of three to make a Tumbling Block. Then the Tumbling Blocks are joined in rows to complete the quilt. The spectacular results are well worth the extra effort. In this version of the *Nine Patch Diamond* there are three values: light, medium, and dark. The medium is really three different pieces of fabric. These three fabrics give dimension to the tumbling blocks that surround the stars, while the stark difference between the light and dark emphasize the star center. Like the previous pattern, *Nine Patch Diamond* is perfect for scrap fabrics, as long as the fabrics are the full width of 42"– 45". The *Nine Patch Diamond* is an extremely versatile pattern. The large number of pieces in a block provide many different arrangements of colors and prints. In this version, the quilt has straight edges and a wide border with contrasting binding.

BLOCK SIZE

Tumbling Blocks made from three Nine Patch Diamonds
   Straight edge to straight edge: 9"
   Point to point: 10¼"
Pieces and corresponding strip sizes
   Piece A: Cut from a strip unit made from three 2"
      strips—yields 16 pieces
   Piece B: Used only to mark matching dots on the completed Nine Patch Diamond blocks

PIECING DIRECTIONS

1. Cut the number of strips required for the quilt size of your choice.

2. Make the pattern template of the pieces. Use a lightweight transparent plastic for scissor-cut pieces, or use with a rotary ruler. This pattern is suited to rotary cutting.

3. Join the strips to make the three-strip strata. There are three color combinations.

Strata 1 is light–dark–medium. Strata 2 is dark–medium–dark. Strata 3 is medium–dark–medium. Press open the seams on the strata. Refer to the yardage and cutting guide for the required number of strata in each combination.

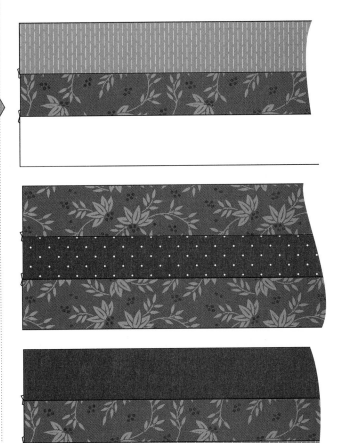

4. The first cut is to angle-cut the strip. To do this place the ruler with template on the strip as illustrated. Make sure the lines in the template match the stitching lines in the strip. The ruler will be at an angle from the corner of the strip. Make

the first cut. Rotate the strip to prepare for cutting the pieces.

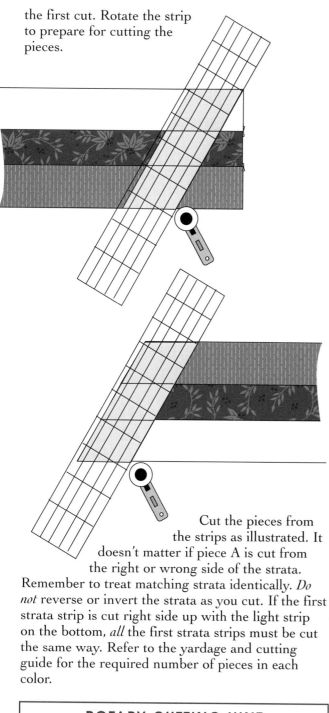

Cut the pieces from the strips as illustrated. It doesn't matter if piece A is cut from the right or wrong side of the strata. Remember to treat matching strata identically. *Do not* reverse or invert the strata as you cut. If the first strata strip is cut right side up with the light strip on the bottom, *all* the first strata strips must be cut the same way. Refer to the yardage and cutting guide for the required number of pieces in each color.

ROTARY CUTTING HINT
Cutting Strata: It is important that the lines on the template match the seams on the strata. To be accurate you need to have a clear view of the template through the rotary ruler. I suggest you use a plain piece of Plexiglas as the straight edge rather than the numbered and grided rulers used for cutting the strip widths.

ROTARY CUTTING HINT
Rotary Cutting Multiple Strip Units: The more fabrics you use in the strips, the more difficult it is to keep the correct color placement as you cut. It is easy at this point to invert the strips. After deciding how the block goes together, you don't want any surprises as you sew. I find it is easiest to cut the strips and maintain the color arrangement if I cut the strips from the right side. Cutting is easier because the seams are clearly visible and not confused with the seam allowances. Also, cutting right side up allows me to see how the colors will be arranged. As an example, prepare to make the first cut on the second strata. Line up a piece cut from the first strata. Lay it on top of the short end of uncut strata, next to the ruler. Check the color location against your original color layout. Are the correct pieces together? If not, rotate the strata to bring the colors into the proper position. Repeat this step for the third strata, by lining up a piece from the first and second strata next to the ruler.

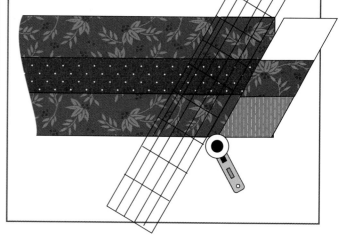

5. Make the required number of nine-patch diamonds. The diamonds are made by sewing together one strip from each strata. Lay out a diamond. Begin by stitching piece 1 to piece 2. There are two matches along this seam. The seam lines in these matches lean in

MATCHING HINT

More Flag Matches: The fastest method is to start the seam with a needle-down start and simply assume the matches will be correct. This is a large assumption, but the method will be moderately successful if the strata were accurately stitched and the pieces carefully cut.

The second method uses the seam allowance flags. When the pieces are rotary cut there are no seam allowance flags. But when you tip up the longer seam allowance on the matching seams, there will be a small triangle of fabric extending beyond the seam edge. Match up the flag triangles from the lower and upper pieces to assure a perfect match. Pin the matches, pinning only into the block, not the seam allowances. This way the seam can be stitched as an open seam. Combine with the needle-down start for super accurate matches. For a further explanation of flag matches see the matching hint in the section, *Stars and Bars*.

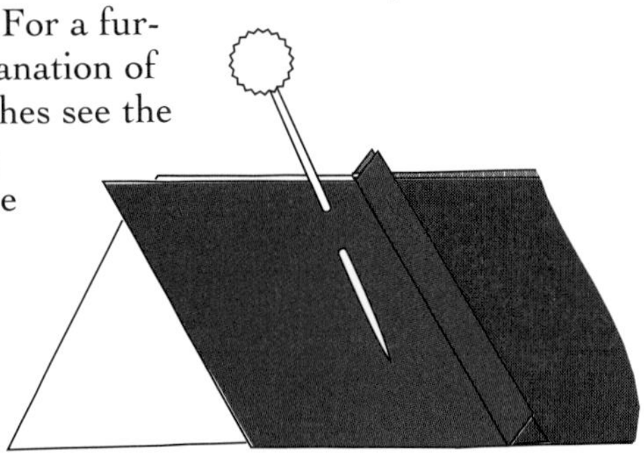

opposite directions, so keyed matches will not work. The matches must be handled one of two ways.

6. Press open all seams. Press carefully. The raw edges of the block are on the bias.

Mark the matching dots on the completed nine-patch diamonds. Use template B to mark the dots on the 120-degree corners of the diamonds. Mass-marking may not work on this diamond. The diamonds may not be all the exact same size, and the seam allowances make it difficult to accurately layer the pieces. Plus, the diamonds may not perfectly match the template. *You can expect slight discrepancies.* Usually the blocks are not uniformly mis-sized. They may be longer and narrower, or wider and shorter. You can correct minor differences as you sew and press the block.

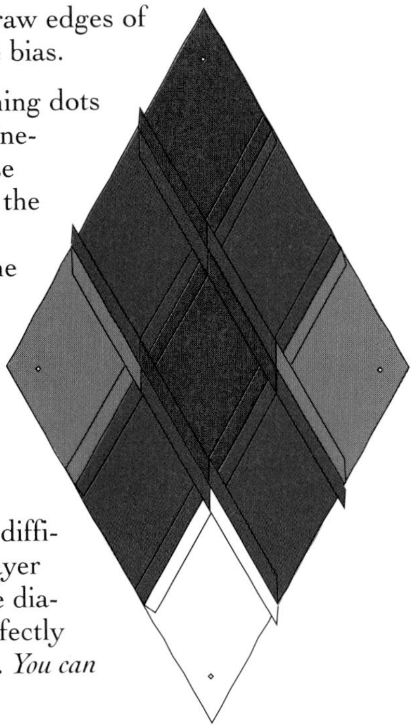

7. Join the nine-patch diamonds to make the Tumbling Blocks. Place the correct edges of the diamonds together to achieve the overall design. Join as illustrated. From the right side the light diamond should be the lower right corner of the left diamond, and the upper right corner of the right diamond. There are two matches along this seam. Use the modified key match to ensure perfect matches. Or simply assume the seams will match when the edges of the piece are lined up. Stitch together two diamonds to bracket the inset. The seam must start exactly on the matching dot on the 120-degree angle. Make a secure knot and sew across the seam and off the edge of the pieces. Press open the seams.

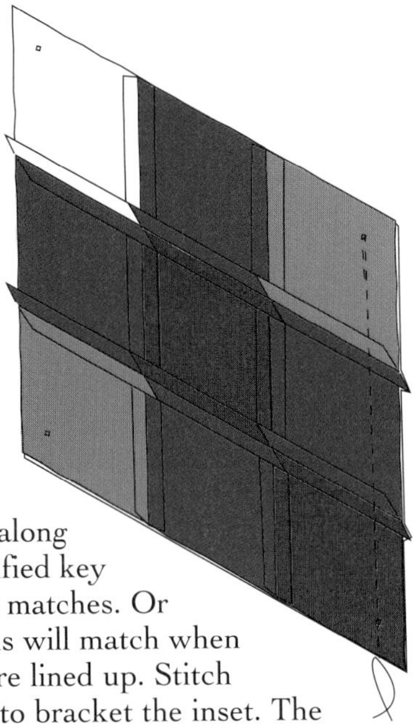

8. Inset the third diamond into the two pieces. Join as illustrated. Match the light diamond to the medium diamond on the left edge of the block. Start and stop sewing at the edge of the fabric. Press open the seam. Refer to the yardage and cutting guide for the required number of complete Tumbling Blocks.

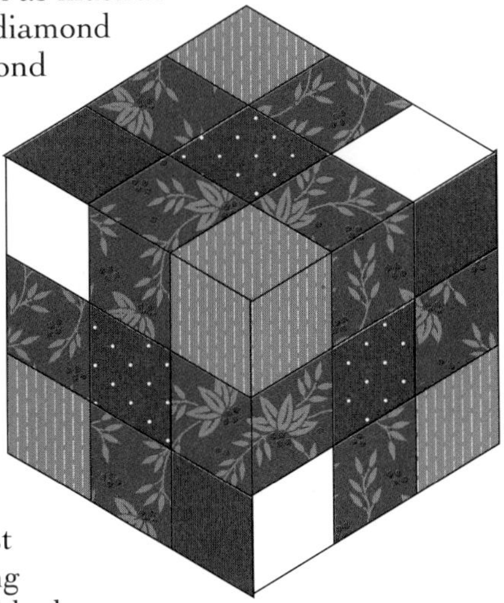

9. Lay out the first row of Tumbling Blocks, placing the blocks *wrong* side up. The first row and all odd rows are always a row of full Tumbling Blocks. The second row and all even rows start with a partial block. The illustration shows a portion of the layout used in the sample. Join all the blocks in this row following the basic instructions for row construction. Use modi-

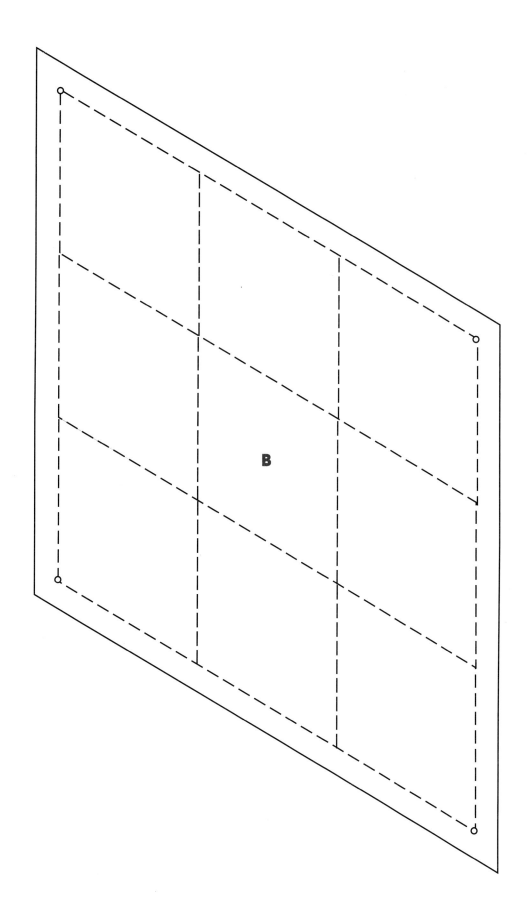

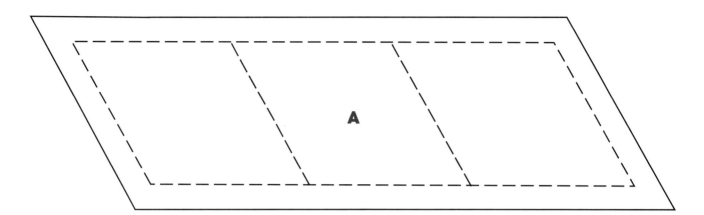

fied key matches for this seam. The seam allowance have been omitted for clarity but the pieces are shown wrong side up. See the marking hint *Matches for Tumbling Blocks* in the previous section, *Colombian Star.*

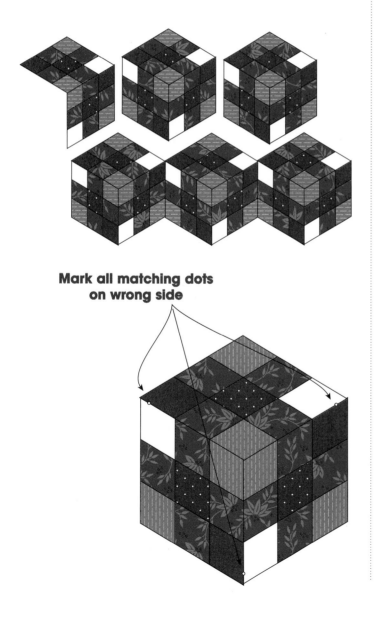

Mark all matching dots on wrong side

10. Lay out the second row of Tumbling Blocks. The second row begins and ends with a partial Tumbling Block as shown in the illustration. Use only two diamonds to make each partial block. When making the partial Tumbling Block, simply sew from edge to edge. This is not an inset seam.

11. Join the blocks of the second row to the first following the basic instructions for row construction.

12. Lay out the remaining rows and join the pieces to the quilt body following the basic row instructions.

13. The partial blocks on the four quilt edges must be cut to make the quilt edge straight. The long edges are simply cut even with the straight edges of the majority of the edge. The top and bottom edges must be cut in a horizontal diamond. Remember the cut edge is

matching dots

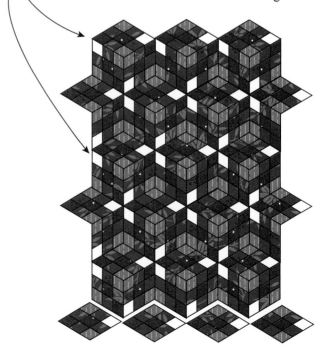

¼" beyond the exact center of the block. Use a 24" ruler and place the ¼" mark of the ruler over the block centers. In this quilt the center falls through the corners of the Tumbling Blocks. Use a fabric marker to mark along the ruler edge. (To be on the safe side, I don't recommend novice quilters cut the blocks until after the border is stitched in place. The experienced quilter may choose to rotary-cut the quilt edge as it is measured.) Straighten the quilt as illustrated.

14. Cut the borders from the required yardage. Cut four strips 9½" wide by the required length. The four border strips will be the measure of the longest side plus 1". The borders can have butted or mitered corners.

15. Mark the quilting design on the quilt top. Choose a border pattern from the selection in Quilting Patterns for Borders.

16. The quilting design is continuous curve. It is not possible to diagram the entire quilt top. Shown is a single block.

17. Stitch the backing together and prepare the quilt for quilting. Layer and baste the quilt.

18. Quilt the quilt and finish with ½"-wide French bias binding.

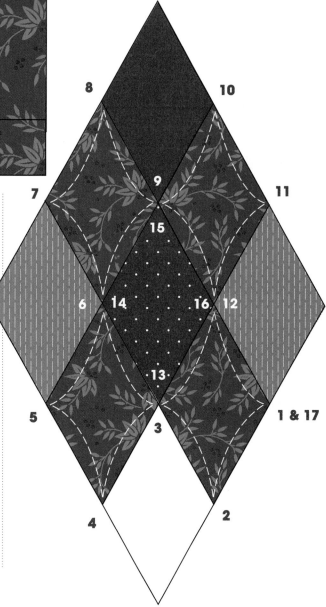

Nine Patch Diamond variation

Nine Patch Diamond Information

	Crib	Twin	Double	Queen	King
Finished size	45" × 57"	72" × 87"	81" × 95"	99" × 103"	108" × 111"
Border width	9"	9"	9"	9"	9"
Block set	3 × 5	6 × 9	7 × 10	8 × 11	10 × 12
Number of blocks	15	54	70	88	120
Amount of fabric required (in yards)					
Blocks					
Dark fabric	1	2½	3¼	4⅛	5½
Light fabric	⅓	¾	⅞	1	1⅜
Medium (each of three prints)	⅓	¾	⅞	1⅛	1½
Borders with mitered or butted corners	1⅝ yd	2½	2¾	3	3⅛
Backing	3¼	5	5⅜	9	9⅜
Bias binding	⅝	⅞	⅞	⅞	1
Cutting Guide					
Dark strips, 2" strips	16	44	56	72	96
Light strips, 2" strips	4	11	14	18	24
Medium strips, 2" strips (each of three prints)	4	11	14	18	24
Total strata units made in each of the three color combinations	4	11	14	18	24
Total pieces cut from strata (each of three color combinations)	51	173	223	278	377
Total nine patch diamonds	51	173	223	278	377
Total complete Tumbling Blocks (made from three diamonds)	13	50	65	83	114
Total partial Tumbling Blocks (Do not make these blocks until needed.)	4	8	10	10	12
Total single blocks for the quilt bottom	4	7	8	9	11

Quintettes

Quintettes and its companion block, *Ozark Tile*, are unfamiliar to many quilters. The combination of elongated hexagon and squares had its heyday around the turn of the century. The patterns were popular for charm quilts, frequently made from silk scraps and always hand pieced. Usually the piecing was done with the English paper method. The fabric was basted around a paper template and then the individual pieces would be hand-whipped together. The whole process was arduous compared to our rotary-cut and strip-pieced quilts of today. It's little wonder that the pattern went out of vogue. Surprisingly, the piecing is logical and straightforward to stitch on the machine. All the versions are a variation of the row method of construction.

The directions here and in the chart, *Quintettes* Information, at the end of this section, are for small wall hangings, appoximately 24" square. This is the type of pattern that is perfect for a small hanging for two reasons. The piecing looks difficult and is sure to impress your quilting friends. Plus, the small pieces make a charming collection of fabrics. The 20" square wall hanging of *Quintettes* requires approximately 90 pieces for the quilt body, while the *Ozark Tile* takes over 100 pieces for the 20" square. At that rate it would require about *six hundred* pieces just for a baby quilt. Antique quilts in these patterns are often seen in a larger scale for a full-size quilt, but the pattern loses much of its appeal as the pieces become larger. The quilts are finished with a straight edge and narrow border. If you choose, you can add prairie points to finish the binding.

This chapter also offers information on accurately cutting small pieces and a *super* fast and accurate way to mark matching dots that doesn't involve a marker or individually handling each piece!

CUTTING AND MATCHING LESSON

Speedy Marking Method for Matching Dots on Complex Pieces: The pieces in this pattern are a perfect example of common problems that can occur with rotary-cutting small inset pieces: inaccuracy and lack of matching dots.

I find that no matter how carefully I line up the rotary ruler, I still have cutting errors. Frequently the ruler shifts and I end up 1/16" to 1/8" off on the total block. That small amount of error is not uncommon, and on large pieces it is not difficult to ease or stretch the pieces to make them correctly fit together. But this margin of error on small pieces is troublesome. Then after the pieces are cut, I am still faced with marking the matching dots on every piece. The marking has its own problems. The marks may not be accurate. Dark fabrics and prints are hard to mark. The markers can be difficult to remove, and it is a tedious process to individually mark every dot on every piece. The most accurate way to cut and mark the pieces is by hand, an awful prospect! What is needed is a way to combine the best of hand and rotary cutting.

One method solves both problems. It is not mainstream and it wastes some fabric. But it is so accurate and neat that the rest of the quiltmaking process is easier. Based on commerical clothing construction methods, the rotary pieces are cut from paper patterns and the matching dots are marked with a small hole. It sounds unlikely, but try it out before making a judgment. I've used this method excusively for years and found it the fastest, most accurate method I've ever tried.

The method uses basic rulers, template plastic, and #2 pencils. It also requires freezer paper, heavy topstitching or buttonhole thread for use on the machine, and a topstitch needle size 120.

The illustration and directions use the elongated hexagons, piece B, from this pattern. The chart, *Quintettes Information*, shows that you need 40 of piece B. They are cut from five strips, with eight pieces in a strip.

Make an accurate lightweight plastic template of the pattern and mark the matching dots with a 1/16" punch.

Cut a piece of freezer paper 42" long. On one of the long edges draw a straight line 1/4" in from the paper edge. Use this as a guideline and draw the eight hexagons on the paper as illustrated. Draw carefully with a sharp pencil, and mark every matching dot. Using a ruler draw a line 1/4" above the top edge of the pieces and cut. This results in a 42" × 3 1/8" strip of freezer paper

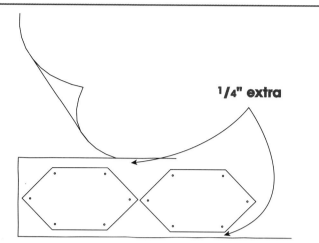

¹/₄" extra

The pieces will be cut and marked one set at a time to maintain the accuracy. Before starting to cut, prepare your machine. Put the topstitch needle in the machine. Thread the machine with topstitch thread in the needle and regular polyester sewing thread in the bobbin. Use the no-bridge embroidery foot, and have the machine in straight stitch, center needle postion.

The first cut separates the first stack of hexagon pieces from the strip. You will cut through all the layers of fabric as you cut between the diagonal ends of the first and second hexagons on the freezer paper strip. Always hold the ruler on the paper template as

marked with eight hexagons.

Cut the fabric strips. The chart, *Quintette Information*, says the strips are 2⅝" wide. For this method every strip *must* be cut about ½" *wider* than the required width. For this pattern cut the strips a generous 3".

The extra width needed to cut the strips can affect the yardage. The five strips at 3" would require slightly over 15". Looking at the yardage I see that it recommends ½ yard, more than enough for the five strips. But the yardage in other patterns is not always ample enough for the extra width. It is best to buy a little extra fabric for this cutting method. It's easy to figure out. Multiply the number of strips required times ½" and add that to the yardage. For example, 8 strips times ½" equals 4". I'd buy an extra ⅛ yard. For a rule of thumb, I routinely buy extra of every fabric in the quilt—usually, ⅛ yard extra for wall hangings, up to ½ yard extra for queen-size quilts. On the average, I find that this method adds about $5–$10 to the cost of a double-size quilt.

you cut, and press down firmly to hold the fabrics in place. After separating the first stack of hexagons from the strip, rotate the mat to cut the remaining sides of the first hexagon. *Carefully* pick up the stack of pieces from the rotary mat. Don't let the pieces shift or fall apart. I strongly recommend a good rotary mat turntable.

Take the stack of five pieces with the freezer paper template on the top to the sewing machine. Place the stack under the presser foot. Align the stack so one matching dot is under the needle. Lower the foot and take *one* stitch through that matching dot. Lift the foot and drag the fabric stack to align the second matching dot under the needle. Take one

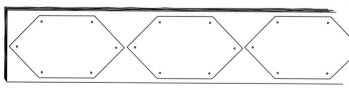

Stack the layers of strips all wrong side up and press with steam. On average, stack five or six layers of fabric strips. More layers of fabric will increase the chance for cutting errors. The steam helps the fabrics stick together and makes the pieces easier to cut. Center the freezer paper strip of hexagons on the top fabric strip, and press it in place.

Continued on page 70

stitch at this matching dot. Continue around the stack taking one stitch at every dot and ending by making the last stitch in the same place as the first. Remove the stack from the machine and leave generous thread tails. Repeat the cutting and stitching process for the eight hexagon stacks.

To mark the stacks of pieces, press the stitched stacks with heavy steam. After steam pressing, the small hole made by the thread is set in the fabric and the pieces can be gently handled and even pressed without the hole closing.

There are a few tips to help you use this marking system:

▼ The fabric stack should be four to eight layers thick. I have successfully used ten-layer stacks, but they can be difficult to cut accurately.

▼ Leave the stacks sewn together until you need the pieces. Then remove the pieces from the stacks as they are used.

▼ To use the pieces, clip the bobbin threads and pull the pieces from the bottom of the stacks.

▼ To clearly see the dots, hold the piece up to a light source like the pool of light from your sewing machine lightbulb that surrounds the presser foot. The matching dot will be a bright pinpoint of light in the dull fabric. The dot is visible from either side of the fabric, on any color or print fabric.

▼ Treat the dots as any other matching dot.

▼ Don't throw away the used freezer paper hexagons, reuse them. The freezer paper hexagons can be re-adhered once or twice before losing stickiness. Substitute the individual hexagons for the freezer paper strip. Place the individual freezer paper hexagons on the fabric stacks and press in place. Rotary-cut as in the previous steps. On large projects recycling the paper pattern saves both freezer paper and time.

Stitching the marking dots is extremely versatile and can be used without using the freezer paper to cut the pieces. This marking method can be combined with a number of cutting methods, including hand cutting and traditional rotary cutting. To use with traditional rotary cut pieces, first, cut the required number pieces in the traditional way. Then stack the pieces, four to ten layers, lining up the edges. Finally, place a paper template over the stack and mark with the stitching.

In other variations, the hexagons and matching dots can be hand traced directly onto the top layer of the fabric stack. This works well with light colored fabrics. Light colored fabrics are easy to mark and the marks are highly visible. The fabric stacks can be cut with a rotary-cutter or scissors.

MARKING HINT

Rubber Stamp for Small Pieces: My favorite way to mark the hexagons is with a rubber stamp. The stamp precludes having to hand trace the pattern to the paper or fabric strips and saves an unbelievable amount of time when working with a large amount of pieces. Most office supply stores can make inexpensive rubber stamps in any shape. The stamp can be made from an accurate copy of the pattern. The copy of the pattern should including the cutting lines and matching dots. I usually request a simple un-inked stamp on a wooden block and handle because it is the least expensive. You can request a pre-inked stamp at a slightly higher cost. Any ink can be used on the freezer paper, including the permanent inks used in pre-inked stamps. The rubber stamp can also be used to mark the fabric. Use an un-inked stamp and washable ink and ink pads available at most rubber stamp stores. This method works best on light colored fabrics because the inks mark more clearly on light colors. There is a large color assortment of washable inks made for children's use. These inks are designed to be easily removed from fabric. It is still a good idea to pretest the ink color to ensure its washability. Don't forget that heat from your iron can set some colors and brands of ink so do not press the samples before trying to remove the marks.

BLOCK SIZE

Small square is 1½"

Elongated hexagon is 2⅛" × 4¼"

Pieces and corresponding strip sizes

Piece A, small square: 2" strip—yields 21 pieces

Piece B, elongated hexagon: 2⅝" strip—yields 8 pieces

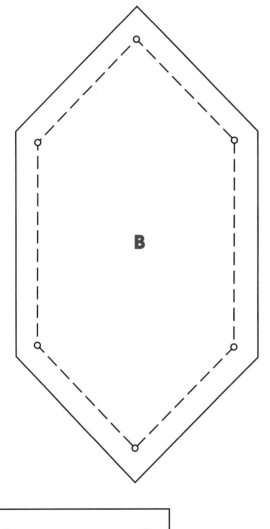

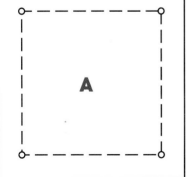

PIECING DIRECTIONS

1. Cut the pieces from the strips as illustrated. Refer to the yardage and cutting guide for the required number of pieces in each color.

2. *Quintettes* are made in units that are joined like *Tumbling Blocks*. The units are constructed with four pieces—two elongated hexagons and two squares.

To make the units, stitch together the two elongated hexagons. Join the hexagons on the long edges as shown. These seams are all inset seams and should stop and start at the matching dots. Press open the seams.

Inset the two squares into the unit. These seams should start and stop at the fabric edge. Press open the seams. Make 18 units.

3. Lay out the first row of units wrong side up. The seam allowances in the illustration have been omitted for clarity, but the pieces are to be placed wrong side up in this order. Join all the blocks in this row following the basic instructions for row construction (see Basic Piecing Method at the beginning of this chapter). These seams are all inset seams and should stop and start at the matching dots.

4. Lay out the second row units. The second row begins and ends with a partial unit as shown in the illustration. Note the right and left units are mirror images. Use only one elongated hexagon and two squares to make each partial unit. When making the partial unit, simply sew from edge to edge as these are not inset seams.

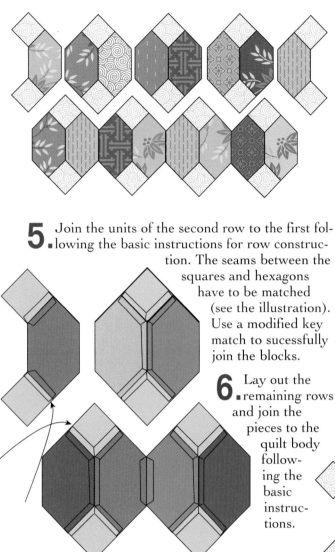

edge is in the middle of the squares. Remember to add ¼" for the seam allowance. Use a fabric marker to mark along the ruler edge. (To be on the safe side, I don't recommend novice quilters cut the blocks until after the border is stitched in place. The experienced quilter may choose to rotary-cut the quilt edge as it is measured.) Straighten the quilt as illustrated.

9. Cut the borders from the required yardage. Cut four strips 2½" wide; the borders are cut crossgrain. The borders have mitered corners.

10. Mark the quilting design on the quilt top using a pattern from the chapter, Quilting Patterns for Pieced Quilts).

11. The quilting design is continuous curve. This pattern can be worked in rows across the quilt. The first illustration shows the first row in both the squares and diamonds. The second illustration shows the completed rows.

12. Stitch the backing together and prepare the quilt for quilting. Layer and baste the quilt.

13. Quilt the quilt.

5. Join the units of the second row to the first following the basic instructions for row construction. The seams between the squares and hexagons have to be matched (see the illustration). Use a modified key match to sucessfully join the blocks.

6. Lay out the remaining rows and join the pieces to the quilt body following the basic instructions.

7. Add the single squares to complete the top and bottom edge of the quilt body.

8. The partial blocks on the four quilt edges must be cut to make the quilt edge straight. On the two long sides the quilt edge is equal to the edges of the hexagons. Line up the ruler with the edges of the hexagons to locate the straight edge. On the top and bottom, the quilt

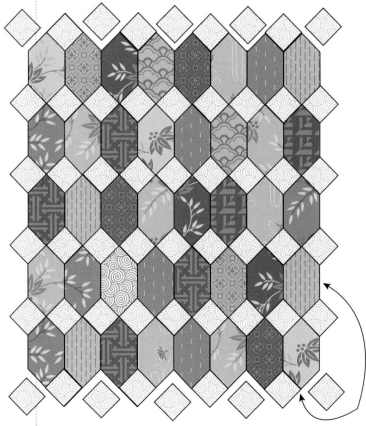

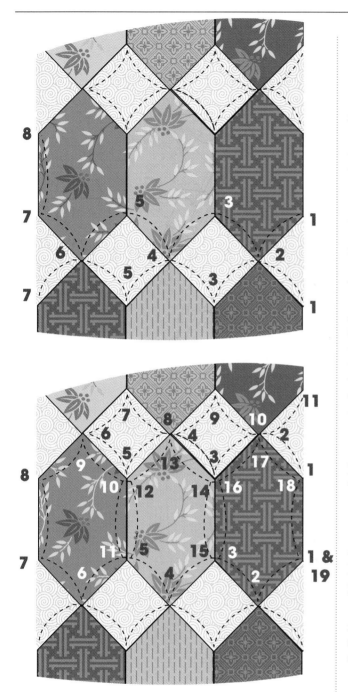

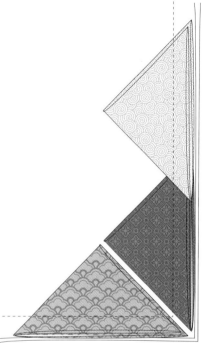

edges. Place them on the right side of the quilt. Line up the raw edges of the prairie point with the raw edges of the quilt top. Evenly distribute the points around the quilt. The points may have to be slightly overlapped to fit the length. Refer to the chart, *Quintettes* Information, for the recommended number of prairie points on each side of the quilt. Pin them securely.

16. Stitch the prairie points along the quilt edges. Use a ¼" seam allowance.

17. Add the rod pocket. Cut one strip 12" × 21" from the backing fabric. Hem the 12" ends with a small hem. Fold the rod pocket in half lengthwise, right sides out.

Center the pocket on the quilt back. Line up the raw edges of the rod pocket with the top of the quilt. Machine-baste the pocket in place with a ¼" seam.

18. Cut the bias binding 1½" wide. Stitch a mock binding (see Quilter's Schoolhouse). Position the binding strip on top of the prairie points, lining up the raw edges. Stitch with a generous ¼" seam allowance.

19. Turn the binding to the quilt back and handstitch in place. Hand blindstitch the lower edge of the pocket to the quilt back.

14. Cut the prairie points. Rotary-cut 3½" squares. Cut 44 squares. To make the prairie point, fold the square in half diagonally. Press. Fold the resulting triangle in half again, lining up the raw edges. Press.

15. Place the points around the quilt

Quintettes Information	
Finished size	21" × 25"
Border width	2½"
Block set	8 × 5
Number of pieces	94
Number of prairie points per side	10 × 12

Amount of fabric required (in yards)

Blocks	
Dark prints, elongated hexagon, piece B	½
Light prints or solid, squares, piece A	¼
Light prints or solids, prairie points	½
Borders (cross cut) with mitered corners	⅓
Backing and rod pocket	⅝
Binding (straight of grain, cross cut)	⅛

Cutting Guide

Elongated hexagons piece B, 2⅝" strips assorted fabric, to equal 42" wide (3⅛" strips if using freezer paper cutting and marking method)	5
Total piece B	40
Squares piece A, 2" strips assorted fabric, to equal 42" wide (2½" strips if using the freezer paper cutting and marking method)	3
Total piece A	54
Total complete units (made from two elongated hexagons and two squares)	18
Total partial units (Do not construct these blocks until needed.)	4

Ozark Tile

Block size

Elongated hexagon is 2⅛" × 4¼"

Square is 2⅛"

Pieces and corresponding strip sizes

Piece B, elongated hexagon: 2⅝" strip—yields 8 pieces

Piece C, square: 2⅝" strip—yields 16 pieces

PIECING DIRECTIONS

1. Cut the required number of pieces from the strips, as illustrated. Refer to the yardage and cutting guide for the required number of pieces in each color.

2. Mark all matching dots.

3. *Ozark Tile* is made in units that are joined like *Tumbling Blocks.* The units are constructed with four elongated hexagons and one square. They are made in two color combinations. Eight are light hexagons with dark center squares, and eight are dark hexagons with light center squares.

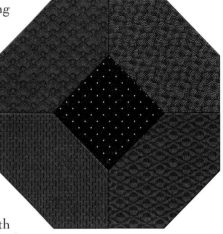

To make the units, stitch together the two elongated hexagons. Join the hexagons on the short edges as shown. Only one edge of this seam is an inset seam. The seam should start at the matching dot on the inset side. Then stitch the seam and off the fabric edge on the opposite side. Press open the seams.

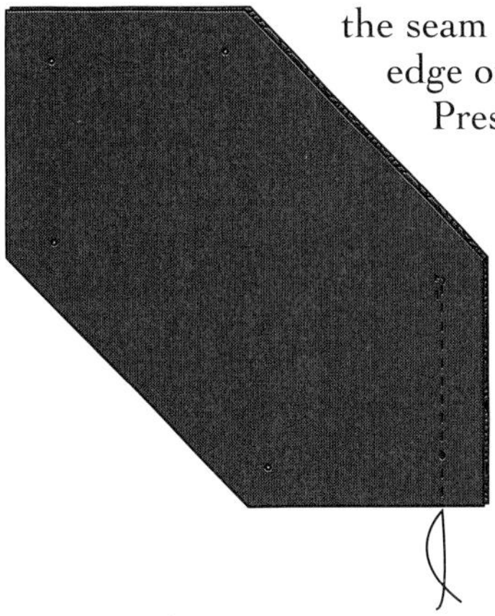

Inset the square into the unit. These seams are all inset seams and should start and stop at the matching dots. Press open the seams. Make 28 units.

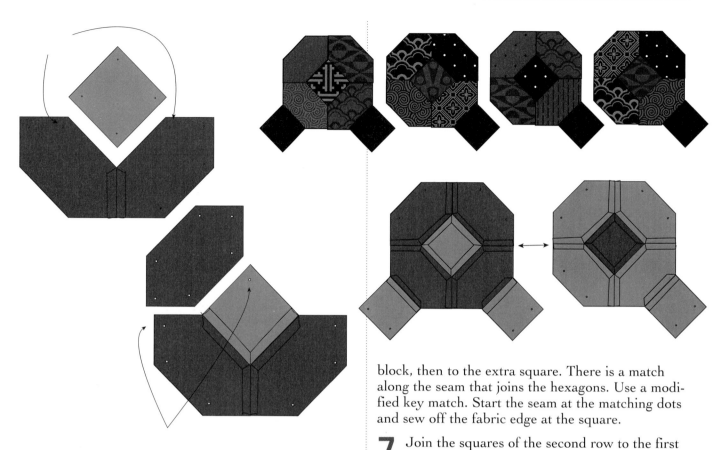

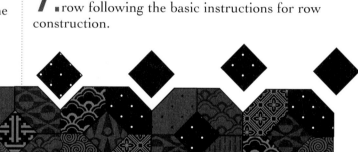

4. Join the third hexagon with an inset seam. The piece will be inset on two sides. The seam should start on the fabric edge when joining the two hexagons, and stop at the matching dot on the square.

Join the fourth hexagon with an inset seam. This piece will be inset on three sides. The seam should start and end on the fabric edge, not on the matching dots.

5. Add the extra squares on the blocks to make the bottom edge of the quilt.

6. Join the blocks in the first row. The blocks will be inset on two sides—first, to the previous

block, then to the extra square. There is a match along the seam that joins the hexagons. Use a modified key match. Start the seam at the matching dots and sew off the fabric edge at the square.

7. Join the squares of the second row to the first row following the basic instructions for row construction.

8. Lay out the remaining rows and join the pieces to the quilt body following the basic instructions.

9. Add the single squares to complete the top and bottom edge of the quilt body.

10. The partial blocks on the four quilt edges must be cut to make the quilt edge straight. Line up the ruler with the edges of the hexagons to locate the straight edge. Use a fabric marker to mark along the ruler edge. (To be on the safe side, I don't recommend novice quilters cut the blocks until after the border is stitched in place. The experienced quilter may choose to rotary-cut the quilt

edge as it is measured.) Straighten the quilt as illustrated.

11. Cut the borders from the required yardage. Cut four strips 2½" wide. The borders are cut cross grain and have mitered corners.

12. Mark the quilting design on the quilt top. Use a border pattern from the chapter, Quilting Patterns for Borders.

13. The quilting design is continuous curve; the stitching sequence is given for one block.

14. Stitch the backing together and prepare the quilt for quilting. Layer and baste the quilt.

15. Quilt the quilt.

16. Add the rod pocket. Cut one strip 12" × 21" from the backing fabric. Hem the 12" ends with a small hem. Fold the rod pocket in half lengthwise, right sides out.

Center the pocket on the quilt back. Line up the raw edges of the rod pocket with the top of the quilt. Machine baste the pocket in place with a ¼" seam.

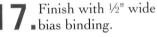

17. Finish with ½" wide French bias binding.

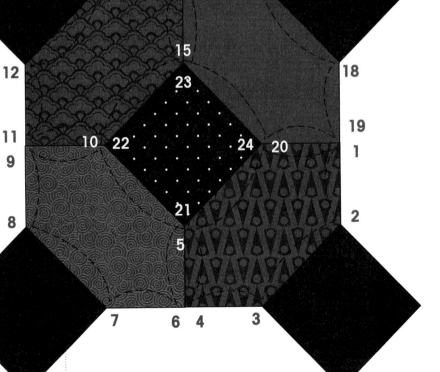

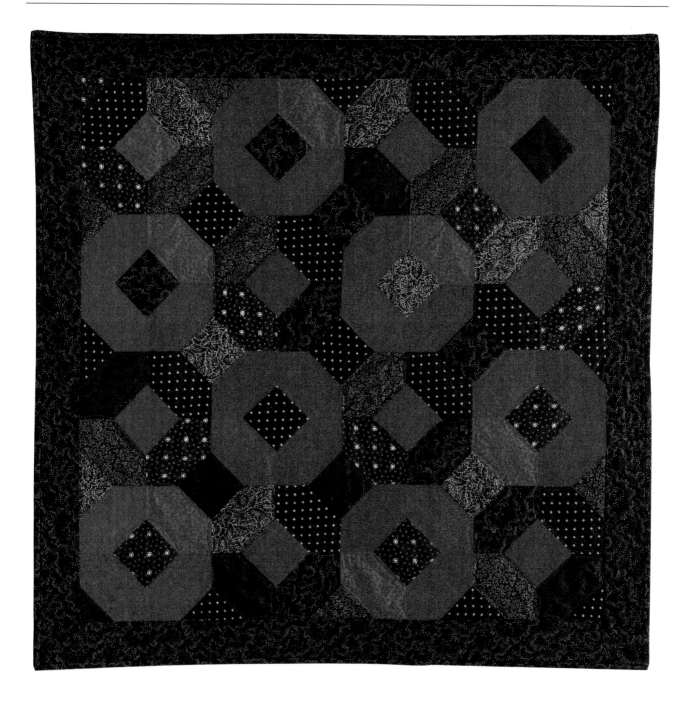

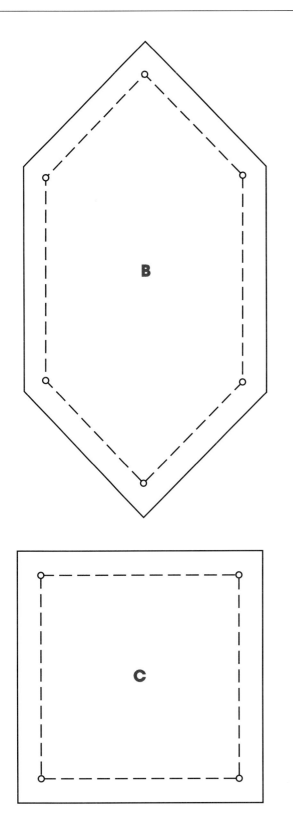

B

C

Ozark Tile Information

Finished size	24" × 24"
Border width	2½"
Block set	8 × 8
Number of pieces	105

Amount of fabric required (in yards)

Blocks
(Purchase ⅛ yard extra of each color if doing freezer paper cutting.)

Light colors, elongated hexagon piece B	½
Dark colors, elongated hexagon piece B	⅝
Light prints or solids, squares piece C	⅛
Dark colors, squares piece C	¼
Borders (cross cut) with mitered corners	⅓
Backing and rod pocket	⅝
Binding (cross cut, straight of grain)	¼

Cutting Guide

(Add ½" to the strip width if using freezer paper cutting.)

Light color, elongated hexagons piece B, 2⅝" strips	4
Dark color, elongated hexagons piece B, 2⅝" strips	4
Total piece B, light color	32
Total piece B, dark color	32
Light color, squares piece C, 2⅝" strips	1
Dark color, squares piece C, 2⅝" strips	3
Total piece C, light color	8
Total piece C, dark color	33
Total complete units (made from two elongated hexagons and two squares)	28
Total partial units (Do not make these blocks until needed.)	8

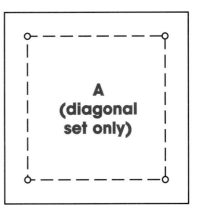

**A
(diagonal
set only)**

Set Variation

There are at least two possible set variations to *Ozark Tiles*. One is the straight set, the other a diagonal set. The sample and previous directions are for the straight set. The straight set uses only two pattern pieces. It is the simplest to lay out, and the most logical place for a beginner to start. The other set to *Ozark Tile* is the diagonal set. It uses the same basic units but gives a totally different effect. Look at the illustration and note how the units are all set on the diagonal.

The diagonal set requires all three pieces of this pattern—the small square A, the large square C, and the hexagon B. This layout requires that the small squares (A) that make the partial blocks on the edge be sewn in place as the row is constructed.

The first row to construct is the middle, longest row. It contains four block units. Add extra squares to the first and last block units to complete the corners of the quilt.

Next add the rows of squares on either side of the central row.

Then add the partial blocks and two full blocks for the next rows on either side of the central row.

Complete the quilt by adding the squares and partial blocks to complete the quilt.

I have included the yardage and general set information for this variation, but have not repeated the basic instructions from the previous sample. Construct this version using the basic *Ozark Tile* directions.

Diagonal Set Information

Finished size	Approximately 24" × 24"
Border width	2½"
Number of pieces	76

Amount of fabric required (in yards)

Blocks
  (Purchase ⅛ yard extra of each color
    if doing freezer paper cutting.)

Dark color, elongated hexagon piece B	⅝
Light prints or solids, squares piece C and A	¼
Borders (cross cut) with mitered corners	⅓
Backing and rod pocket	⅝
Binding (cross cut, straight of grain)	1/4

Cutting Guide

  (Add ½" to strip width if doing freezer
    paper cutting.)
Dark color, elongated hexagons piece B

2⅝" strips	6
Total piece B	40
Light color, squares piece C, 2⅝" strips	1
Total piece C	16
Light color, squares piece A, 2" strips	1
Total piece A	20
Total complete units	8
Total partial units made from one hexagon and two squares	8

Interlocking Motif Designs

Texas Stars and *Grandmother's Flower Garden* are constructed as interlocking hexagons. These designs are based on the hexagon block but the blocks share common background pieces. Interlocking hexagons form a more compact pattern than row set hexagons. Notice the difference between the two illustrations below. In one design the stars are individual blocks and the quilt is constructed using the basic row method. In the other, the stars share a background diamond. The design with the shared diamonds is the interlocking pattern. Like the row method of construction, the hexagon units are added one at a time to the previous rows.

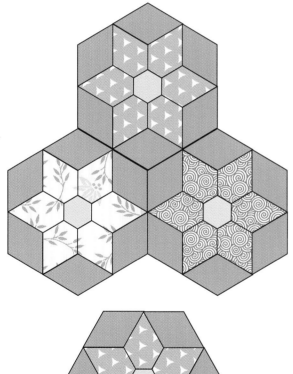

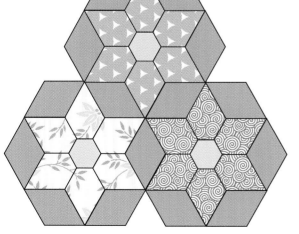

Texas Stars

Texas Stars is an interlocking motif, and is an introduction to both interlocking designs and motif constructions. The basic block is a hexagon formed by a six-point star with diamond edges. The shared background pieces give the appearance of overlapping blocks. The patterns have less background, and with careful color selection can have many layers of designs. Traditionally, Texas Stars are made from two values, light and medium: see my smaller variation quilt, shown on page 111. The background diamonds and star centers are light, while the star points are made from an assortment of medium prints. A completely different effect could be achieved by placing light stars on a dark background. For added interest I used a selection of 30s fabrics for the star points. The pattern makes an easy straight edge, and the sample is finished with a border and striped binding. The pattern directions are for one size—46" × 56".

BLOCK SIZE

Basic block is 8½" wide by 10" long

Pieces and corresponding strip sizes

Piece A, hexagon: 2½" strip—yields 14 pieces

Piece B, star points: 2⅞" strip—yields 14 pieces

Piece C, background diamond: 2½" strip—yields 13 pieces

PIECING DIRECTIONS

1. Cut the required number of pieces from each of the fabrics. Refer to the yardage and cutting guide for the required number of pieces in each color. The pieces may be cut and marked in any method you choose. Mark all the matching dots on every piece. I recommend the freezer paper cutting and stitch marking explained in the previous chap-

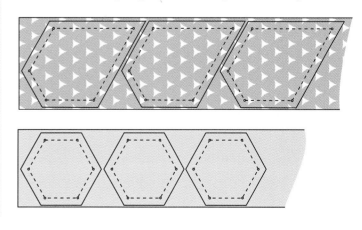

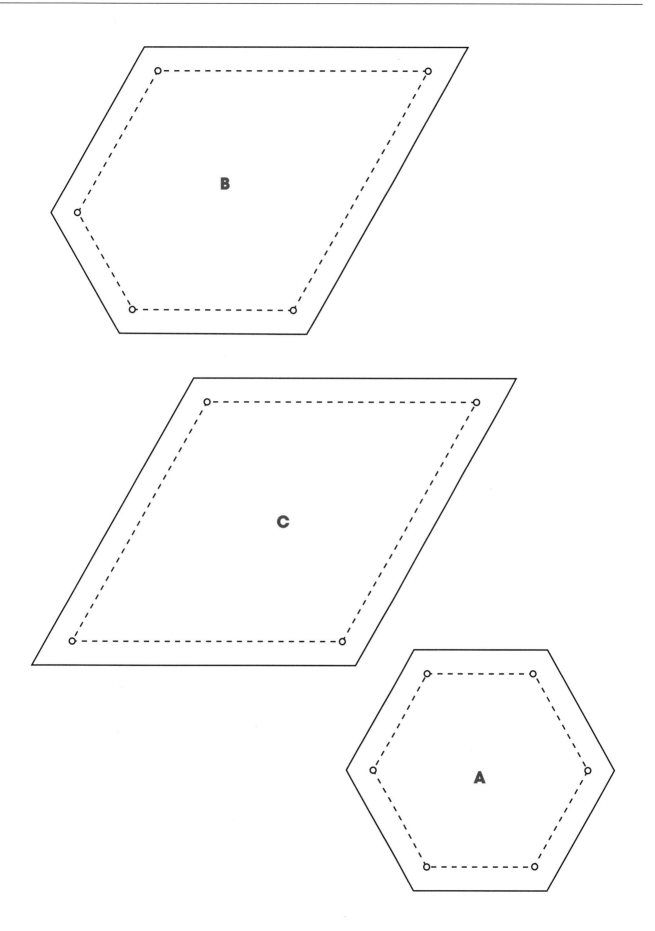

PIECING HINTS

Basic Hexagon Motif Construction: Motifs like the *Texas Stars* and *Grandmother's Flower Garden* always start in the center, and the pieces are stitched in rings rather than rows. Like the row construction, the pieces are added one at a time to the center.

Begin by placing the first star point and the star center right sides together. The first seam will join the base of the star point to the center. It is similar to joining the first two hexagons in the row construction. Press open the seam.

Place the two pieces *wrong side up* on a flat surface. Think of the star as a clock face. The first piece, in this example the star point, should be at twelve o'clock and the center is the

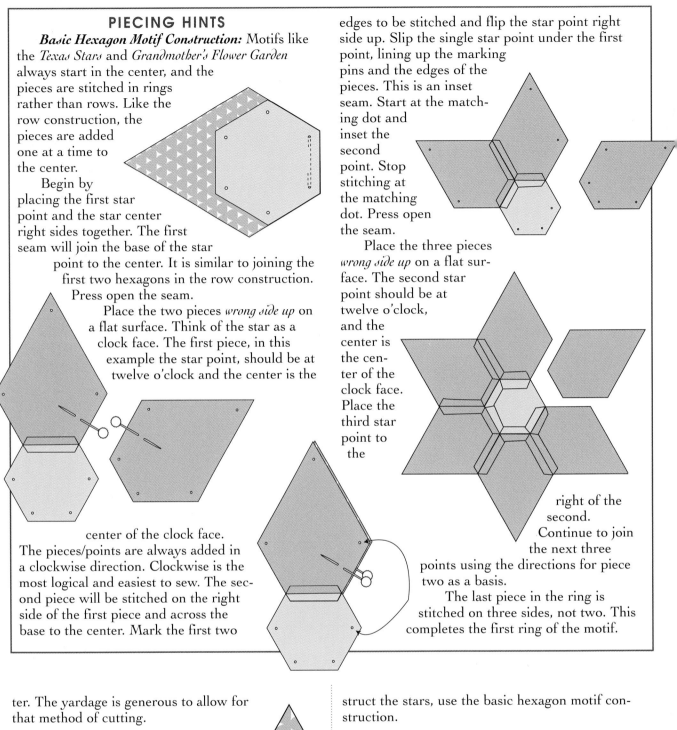

center of the clock face. The pieces/points are always added in a clockwise direction. Clockwise is the most logical and easiest to sew. The second piece will be stitched on the right side of the first piece and across the base to the center. Mark the first two

edges to be stitched and flip the star point right side up. Slip the single star point under the first point, lining up the marking pins and the edges of the pieces. This is an inset seam. Start at the matching dot and inset the second point. Stop stitching at the matching dot. Press open the seam.

Place the three pieces *wrong side up* on a flat surface. The second star point should be at twelve o'clock, and the center is the center of the clock face. Place the third star point to the

right of the second. Continue to join the next three points using the directions for piece two as a basis.

The last piece in the ring is stitched on three sides, not two. This completes the first ring of the motif.

ter. The yardage is generous to allow for that method of cutting.

2. Texas Stars are made in units. The units are constructed with six star points, one star center, and three diamonds. The star seams are inset seams and start and stop at the matching dots. To con-

struct the stars, use the basic hexagon motif construction.

3. Inset the diamonds on three sides of the star, as illustrated. These seams will not be used for insets and can be stitched from edge to edge as a normal seam. Press open all seams.

4. Make the required blocks and partial blocks:

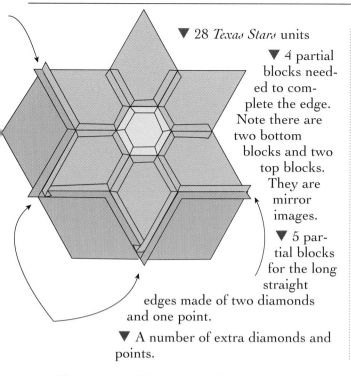

▼ 28 *Texas Stars* units

▼ 4 partial blocks needed to complete the edge. Note there are two bottom blocks and two top blocks. They are mirror images.

▼ 5 partial blocks for the long straight edges made of two diamonds and one point.

▼ A number of extra diamonds and points.

5. Lay out the units for the first row. Place six units wrong side up on a flat surface. (The illustration does not show the seam allowances to keep the diagram clearer and less cluttered.) This first row will make one long edge of the quilt. To complete the straight edge will require seven extra point pieces. Place these in the correct location.

6. Stitch two star point pieces to the first unit. These seams will not be used for inset and can be stitched from edge to edge as with a normal seam. The matching dots can be used to line up the pieces. Press open the seams.

7. Stitch one extra star point piece to each of the remaining units in the first row. Press open the seams.

8. Join the first unit to the second. Sew with the first unit on top, the second unit on the bottom. These are not inset seams and can be sewn edge to edge. There are two matches where the star points

TOP

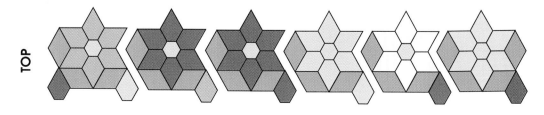

TOP

meet—one at the beginning of the seam, the other in the middle of the second half of the seam. Use a stab pin and the matching dots, or match the seam allowance flags for perfectly matched points. Press open the seams.

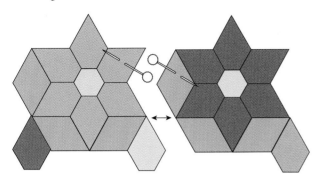

9. Join the remaining units in the first row using the directions for unit two as a basis. *Always sew with the new single unit on the bottom* and the quilt body on the top. This may seem upside down to you, but it is correct. Finish the first row with an extra diamond to make the straight edge.

10. Lay out the units for the second row, wrong sides up. The first unit in the second row is a partial block. This is not an inset seam and the seam may be sewn from edge to edge. Join the partial block and press open the seams. (The

illustration does not show the seam allowances to keep the diagram clearer and less cluttered.)

11. The second unit in the second row is inset on four sides. There will be four pivots to complete the single seam. The seam can be started on the fabric edge and will end on the fabric edge. Besides the four pivots, there are four star points to match. With practice you won't have to pin the seam if you use the seam allowance flags to help align the match. The beginner might find it easier to stitch with the pivots and matches pinned.

12. Join the remaining units to the second row and end with the partial block.

13. Starting with a whole unit, join the third row like the second.

14. The fifth row requires extra pieces to make a straight edge. Join the extra diamonds and points as illustrated, before joining the units to the quilt body.

15. The partial blocks on the four quilt edges must be cut to make the quilt edge straight. On the two long sides the quilt edge is equal to the edges of the star units. Line up the ruler with the edges of the units to locate the straight edge. On the top and bottom, the quilt edge will be along the points of the stars. Remember to add ¼" for the seam allowance. Use a fabric marker to mark along the ruler edge. (To be on the safe side, I don't recommend novice quilters cut the blocks until after the border is stitched in place. The experienced quilter may choose to rotary-cut the quilt edge as it is measured.) Straighten the quilt as illustrated.

16. Cut the borders from the required yardage. Cut four strips 4" wide by 57" long. The four border strips will be the measure of the longest side plus 1". Attach the borders. The border can have butted or mitered corners.

17. Mark the quilting design on the quilt top.

18. Stitch the backing together and prepare the quilt for quilting.

Layer and baste the quilt. The quilting pattern is a continuous curve design. The illustration shows one block.

19. Quilt the quilt and finish with ½"-wide French bias binding.

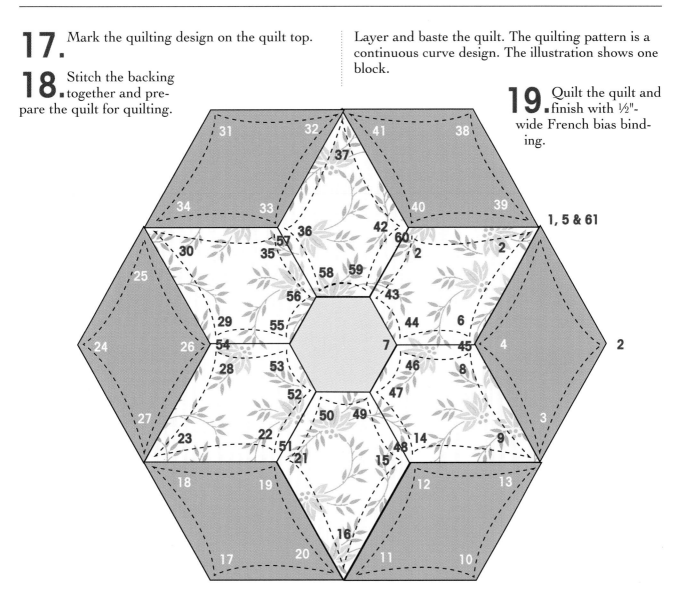

1, 5 & 61

2

Texas Stars Information			
Finished size	46" × 56"	**Cutting Guide**	
Border width	4"	(Add ½" to strip width if doing freezer paper cutting.)	
Block set	5 × 6	Star points, piece B, 2⅞" strips	15
Number of pieces	338	Total piece B	198
Amount of fabric required (in yards)		Hexagon centers, piece A, 2½" strips	3
(The yardage needed for freezer paper cutting is in parentheses.)		Total piece A	32
Blocks		Background diamonds, piece C, 2½" strips	9
Medium prints, star points B1	½ (1¾)	Total piece C	105
Light prints or solid, hexagon center A	¼ (⅝)	Total whole units (made from 1 hexagon center, 6 star points, and 3 diamonds)	28
Light prints or solids, background diamond C	1 (1⅛)		
Borders with mitered corners	1¾	Total partial units for top and bottom (Do not make these blocks until needed.)	4
Backing	1⅝		
Binding	½	Total partial units for the sides	7

Grandmother's Flower Garden

Grandmother's Flower Garden is a charming pattern that uses the diamond and triangle path instead of the more frequently seen hexagon path. Like *Texas Stars*, this version of *Grandmother's Flower Garden* is an interlocking motif pattern. It gives an intricate appearance without much effort. The sample is made from a slightly unconventional color scheme. I've chosen black for the paths and jewel toned solids and prints for the flowers. The effect is like a stained-glass window. The more traditional choice is a green path with multi-colored flowers. I've used an unpieced border. (For an alternative border, I recommend the one in Mimi Dietriche's book *Handmade Quilts*. She has a great pieced border around *Grandmother's Flower Garden*. The border looks like a picket fence. She even uses prairie points to make the pointed tops to the pickets. How clever! It's the perfect border for a garden.) This pattern makes an easy straight edge, and the sample is finished with a border and striped binding. The pattern directions are for one size—36" × 45".

BLOCK SIZE

Basic block is 5" wide by 5¾" long
Pieces and corresponding strip sizes
Piece A, hexagon: 2½" strip—yields 14 pieces
Piece E, path triangle: 1¾" strip—yields 40 pieces
Piece D, path diamond: 1½" strip—yields 23 pieces

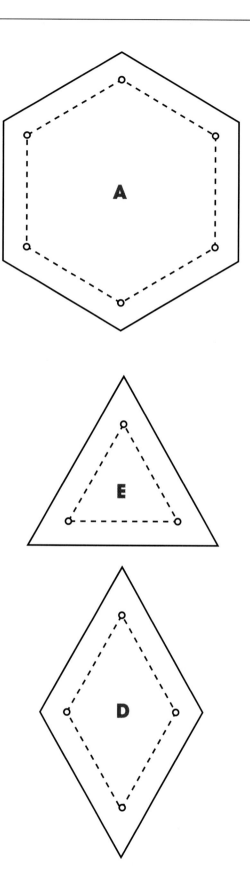

PIECING DIRECTIONS

1. Cut the required number of pieces from each of the fabrics. Refer to the chart, *Grandmother's Flower Garden* Information, at the end of this section, for the required number of pieces in each color. The pieces may be cut and marked in any method you choose. I recommend the freezer paper cutting and stitch marking explained in the lesson in the *Quintettes* chapter. The yardage is generous to allow for that method of cutting.

2. The flowers are made in units. The units are constructed with six hexagon petals, one flower center, three diamonds, and two triangles.

Most seams are inset seams and start and stop at the matching dots.

To construct the flower units, use the basic motif construction: Motifs like in *Grandmother's Flower Garden* always start in the center and the pieces are stitched in rings, rather than rows. Like in row construction, the pieces are added one at a time to the rings. The petals are added in a clockwise direction around the flower center. Construct the flower motif using the basic hexagon construction directions given in the previous section, *Texas Stars*.

3. Inset the three diamonds on the three sides of the unit and join the two triangles as illustrated. These seams will not be inset and can be stitched from edge to edge as a normal seam. Press open all seams.

4. Make the required blocks and partial blocks:

▼ 28 whole flower units

▼ 4 partial blocks needed to complete the edge. Note there are two bottom blocks and two top blocks. They are mirror images.

5. Lay out the units for the first row. Place six units wrong side up on a flat surface as illustrated. This first row will make one long edge of the quilt. To complete the straight edge will require fourteen extra pieces: seven triangles and seven hexagons.

6. Stitch the extra pieces to the first unit. These are not inset seams and can be sewn edge to edge. The matching dots can be used to line up the pieces, or use the seam allowance flags for a perfect match. Press open the seams. In the illustrations the seam allowances have been omitted for clarity. The pieces are placed wrong side up during the layout and stitching process.

7. Stitch the extra pieces to each of the remaining units in the first row. Press open the seams.

8. Join the first unit to the second unit. Sew with the first unit on top, the second unit on the bottom. These will not be inset seams and can be sewn edge to edge. There are three matches along the diamonds. Use a stab pin and the matching dots, or match the seam allowance flags for perfectly matched points. Press open the seams.

used for inset and can be stitched from edge to edge. Besides the four pivots, there are six matches for the diamonds. With practice you won't have to pin the seam, but the beginner might find it easier to stitch with the pivots and matches pinned.

12. Join the remaining units to the second row and end with the partial block.

13. Starting with a whole unit, join the third row like the second.

14. The fourth row requires extra pieces to make a straight edge. Join the extra diamonds and hexagons as illustrated, before joining the units to the quilt body.

15. The partial blocks on the four quilt edges must be cut to make the quilt edge straight. On the two long sides the quilt edge is equal to the edges of the star units. Line up the ruler with the edges of the units to locate the straight edge. On the top and bottom, the quilt edge will divide the diamonds in half. Remember to add ¼" for the seam allowance. Use a fabric marker to mark along the ruler edge. (To be on the safe side, I don't recommend novice quilters cut the blocks until after the border is stitched in place. The experienced quilter may choose to rotary-cut the quilt edge as it is measured.) Straighten the quilt as illustrated.

9. Join the remaining units in the first row using the directions for unit two. *Always sew with the new single unit on the bottom* and the quilt body on the top. This may seem upside down to you, but it is correct. Finish the first row with an extra diamond for the straight edge.

10. The first unit in the second row is a partial block. Join the partial block and press open the seams.

11. The second unit in the second row is inset on four sides. There will be four pivots to complete the single seam. This seam will not be

16. Cut the borders from the required yardage. Cut four strips 5" wide by 46" long. The four border strips will be the measure of the longest side plus 1". Attach the borders. The border can have butted or mitered corners.

17. Mark the quilting design on the quilt top. Choose a pattern from Part II, Machine Quilting. The blocks are quilted in continuous curve.

18. Stitch the backing together and prepare the quilt for quilting. Layer and baste the quilt.

19. Quilt the quilt and finish with ½"-wide French bias binding.

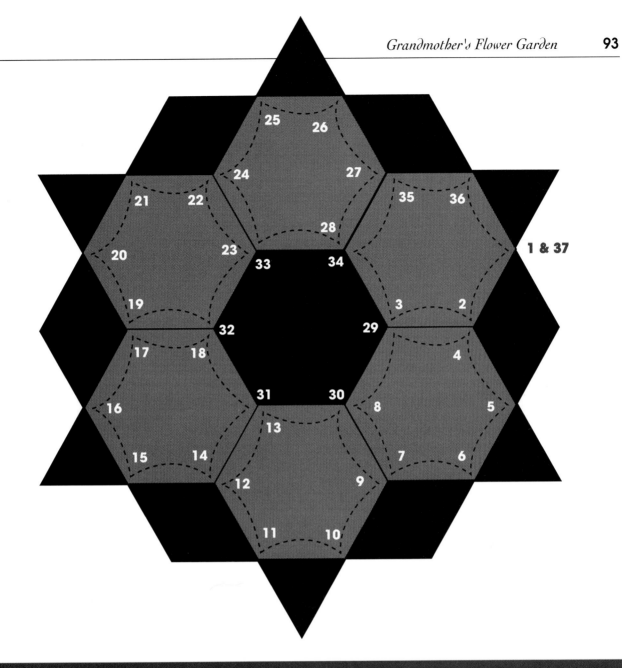

Grandmother's Flower Garden Information

Finished size	36" × 45"	
Border width	5"	
Block set	5 × 6	
Number of pieces	412	

Amount of fabric required (in yards)

(The yardage needed for freezer paper cutting is in parentheses.)

Blocks		
Medium prints or solid, petals A	1⅜ (1½)	
Light prints or solid, hexagon center A	¼ (⅜)	
Dark prints or solid, path diamonds D	⅓ (½)	
Dark prints or solid, path triangles E	¼ (⅜)	
Borders with mitered corners	1⅜	
Backing	1⅜	
Binding	½	

Cutting Guide

(Add ½" to strip width if doing freezer paper cutting.)

Petals piece A, 2½" strips	15
Total piece B	198
Hexagon centers, piece A, 2½" strips	3
Total piece A	32
Path diamonds, piece C, 1½" strips	5
Total piece C	108
Path triangles, piece D, 1¾" strips	2
Total piece D	74
Total whole units (made from 1 hexagon center, 6 hexagon petals, 2 triangles, and 3 diamonds)	28
Total partial units (Do not construct these blocks until needed.)	4

Hexagon Motif-Based Designs

Basic Piecing Method

Texas Stars and *Grandmother's Flower Garden* are basic motif-based designs. They have a single ring of petals around the center hexagon. Most *Grandmother's Flower Garden* blocks are made from multiple rings—a center, one or two rings of petal color, a green ring representing the leaves, and then a neutral-colored path. These round motifs are called rosettes. Other common multi-ring motifs are triangles, diamonds, and stars. There are many variations, and they are usually combined with rosettes for large complex patterns. Traditionally, complex motifs are made from small hexagons, under 1" across. The large number of individual pieces required for a quilt top can create dozens of motifs for the larger complex designs. The more pieces, the more space for the quiltmaker to express his/her ideas and designs. The basic instructions that follow use a simple hexagon block to explain the technique. I suggest you make this three-ring rosette to try out the motif construction.

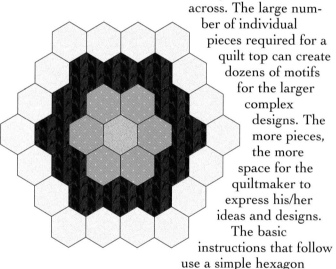

Rosette Motif Construction

The sample can be made from scrap fabrics. For rotary cutting, the strips are 2½" wide. Cut one flower center, six petals for the first ring, twelve petals for the second ring, and eighteen petals for the third ring. The hexagon pieces can be scissor- or rotary-cut, either way it is necessary to mark all the dots on every piece. I recommend the stitch marking explained in the Freezer Paper Lesson in the *Quintettes* section of this chapter.

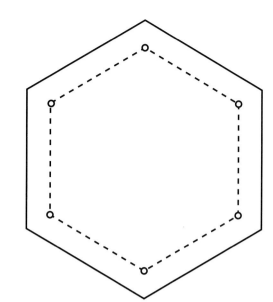

First Ring

1. Cut the required number of pieces from each of the fabrics.

2. Lay out the hexagons in the correct placement. This will give you a clear idea of how the finished rosette will look.

3. The first steps will be joining the first ring to the center. Begin by placing the first petal and the flower center right sides together. The first seam will join the petal to the center, as described in basic row construction at the start of the Hexagons chapter. Press open the seam.

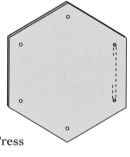

4. Place the two pieces *wrong side up* on a flat surface. Think of the flower as a clock face. The first petal should be at twelve o'clock and the center is the center of the clock face. The petals are always added in a clockwise direction. Clockwise is the most logical and easiest to sew.

5. Place the second petal, wrong side up, to the right of the first at about two o'clock. The second petal is

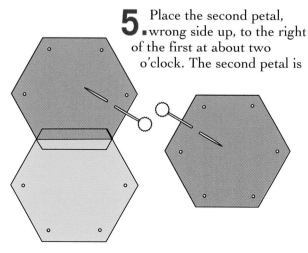

inset on two sides. It will be stitched to first petal and the center. Mark the first two edges to be stitched and flip the petal right side up.

6. Slip a single petal under the first petal, lining up the marking pins and the edges of the pieces. This is an inset seam. Start at the matching dot and inset the second petal. Stop stitching at the matching dot. Press open the seam.

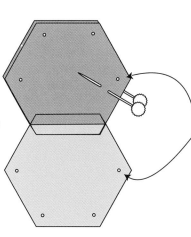

7. Place the three pieces *wrong side up* on a flat surface. The second petal should be at twelve o'clock and the center is the center of the clock face. Place the third petal to the right of the second.

Continue to join the next three petals using the directions for the second petal.

8. The last piece in the ring is inset on three sides, not two. This completes the first ring of the motif.

Second Ring

9. Place the rosette *wrong side up* on a flat surface. The top petal should be at twelve o'clock.

10. The first petal in the second ring is stitched to the top petal, just like the first petal on the first ring was stitched to the center. Press open the seam.

11. Place the rosette *wrong side up* on a flat surface. The first petal in the second ring should be at twelve o'clock.

12. Place the second petal in the second ring, wrong side up, to the right of the first at about two o'clock. The second petal is inset on three sides. It will be stitched to the first petal in the second ring and to the two petals in the first ring.

Mark the first two edges to be stitched and flip the petal right side up.

13. Slip a single petal under the first petal in the second ring, lining up the marking pins and the edges of the pieces. This is an inset seam. Start at the matching dot and inset the second petal. Stop stitching at the matching dot. Press open the seam. This step is similar to joining the second hexagon of the second row in basic row construction.

14. Place the rosette *wrong side up* on a flat surface. The second petal should be at twelve o'clock. Place the third petal to the right of the second. Continue to join the next nine petals using the directions for the second petal.

15. The last piece in the ring is inset on four sides. This completes the second ring of the motif.

Remaining Rings

16. Every ring after the first ring is stitched in exactly the same way. Use the directions for the second ring to complete the third ring.

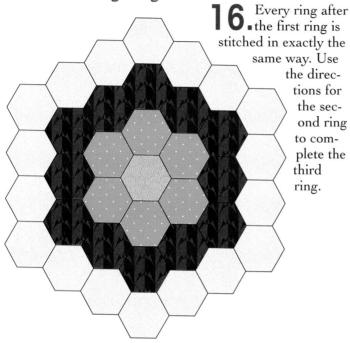

Diamond Motif Construction

The sample can be made from scrap fabrics. For rotary cutting the strips are 2½" wide. Cut one flower center, eight hexagons for the first ring, and sixteen hexagons for the second ring. The hexagon pieces can be scissor- or rotary-cut. Either way it is necessary to mark all the dots on every piece. I recommend the stitch marking explained in the Freezer Paper Lesson in the *Quintettes* section of this chapter.

First Ring

1. Repeat the first ring directions from the rosette motif, steps 1 through 8.

2. To make the diamond shape requires two extra diamonds on each side of the rosette. Place the rosette *wrong* side up on a

flat surface. The top hexagon should be at twelve o'clock. The two additional hexagons are added at three o'clock and nine o'clock. They are inset on two sides.

Second Ring

3. Place the diamond *wrong* side up on a flat surface. The top hexagon should be at twelve o'clock. The first hexagon in the second ring is stitched to the top hexagon, just as the first hexagon on the first ring was stitched to the center. Press open the seam.

4. Place the diamond *wrong* side up on a flat surface. The first hexagon in the second ring should be at twelve o'clock.

5. Place the second hexagon in the second ring, wrong side up, to the right of the first hexagon at about two o'clock. The second hexagon is inset on three sides. It will be stitched to the first hexagon in the second ring and to the two hexagons in the first ring. Mark the first two edges to be stitched and flip the hexagon right side up.

6. Slip a single hexagon under the first hexagon in the second ring, lining up the marking pins and the edges of the pieces. This is an inset seam. Start at the matching dot and inset the second hexagon. Stop stitching at the matching dot. Press open the seam. This step is similar to joining the second hexagon of the second row in basic row construction.

7. Place the diamond *wrong* side up on a flat surface. The second hexagon should be a twelve o'clock. Place the third hexagon to the right of the second.

8. The fourth and fifth hexagons are at the diamond point. The fourth hexagon is inset on

only two sides, while the fifth through tenth are inset on three sides. Continue to add the hexagons to complete the ring. The last piece in the ring is inset on four sides.

9. Two extra hexagons are added to this ring to maintain the diamond shape. This completes the second ring of the motif.

Remaining Rings

10. Every ring after the first ring is stitched in exactly the same way. Use the directions for the second ring to complete the third ring.

Joining Hexagon Motifs

After making the rosettes, it is necessary to join them to make the quilt top. There is one small problem. Look at the edges of the motifs—the seam is a zig-zag seam. Half the insets are at the top, half at the bottom. There are three ways to join this seam.

1. The seam can be hand stitched. That is very accurate, but so slow.

2. The seam can be joined with machine-done insets. In this method every other inset is stitched wrong side up. The illustration clearly shows the problem. On the first inset point the seam for the inset is on the under row of pieces while the point to inset is on the top. That is just the reverse of the usual way to inset pieces. Look at the second inset. Here the pieces are right. The seam for the inset is on the top while the point to be inset is on the bottom. That means you can't see half of the

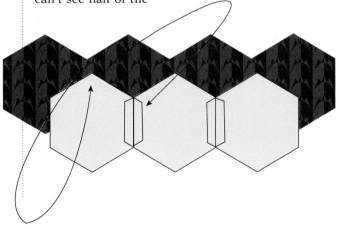

insets you have to stitch to complete the seam. It is possible to successfully use this method. It works reasonably well on large pieces, and of course practice helps. But, I don't think it is worth the effort when there is a much faster and simpler way to join the motifs.

3. The third method is the most practical, fastest, easiest, all around best way to handle the zigzag seams. Simply cut the hexagons on the edges in half. That makes the motif a large hexagon and the motifs can be joined using the row method of construction. This will require two extra pattern pieces: a half hexagon and a third hexagon. They are substituted for the full hexagons on the motif edges. In the following patterns the directions and pattern pieces include the partial hexagons. By using the partial hexagons you can transform complex motifs and even hexagon borders into large, easy-to-join

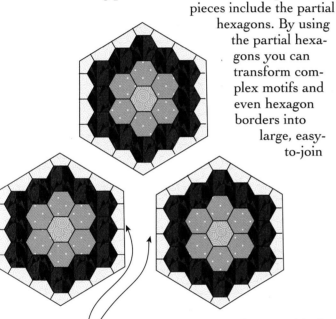

hexagon blocks. The hexagons will have matches along the straight edges, but these are easy to match using a modified key match. It offers the best of both worlds — the look and charm of intricate hexagon piecing with the simplicity of quick-piecing methods.

Rosettes with Hexagon Border

The *Rosettes with Hexagon Border* pattern is probably the most frequently seen version of *Grandmother's Flower Garden*. The basic rosettes are made from three rings with a hexagon path, and there is a hexagon border. Once you understand the basics of motif construction there is a whole world of possibilities. In this pattern the basic motif is expanded to include a hexagon border. The piecing starts with the basic rosette and adds partial rings to make the border. The border is complete when you finish the motifs. I chose a brilliant color scheme that is basically red and cream. The rosettes are made from an assortment of print fabrics. The yardage is given for each ring to help you plan your own version of this classic pattern. The quilt has two straight edges and two irregular edges, a great place to practice binding.

BLOCK SIZE

The basic rosette measures 16" × 14"

Pieces and corresponding strip sizes

Piece A, hexagon: 2½" strip—yields 14 pieces
Piece A1, half hexagon: 2½" strip—yields 24 pieces
Piece A2, third hexagon: 1¾" strip—yields 16 pieces

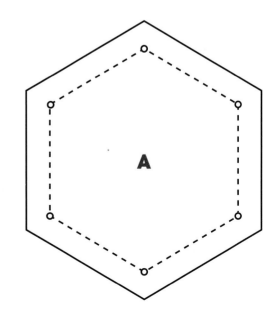

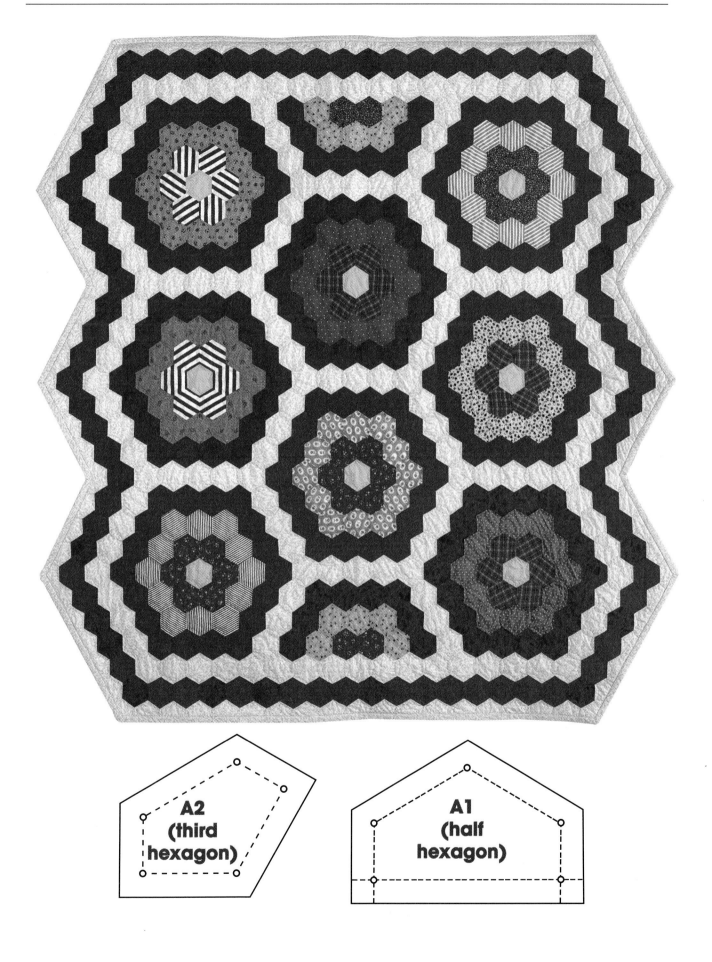

PIECING DIRECTIONS

1. Cut the required number of pieces from each of the fabrics. Refer to the chart, *Rosettes with Hexagon Border* Information, at the end of this section, for the required number of pieces in each color. The pieces may be cut and marked in any method you choose. Mark all the matching dots on every piece. I recommend the freezer paper cutting and stitch marking explained in the Freezer Paper Lesson in the *Quintettes* section of this chapter.

2. There are six basic motifs to this pattern. All these motifs can be stitched using the basic motif instructions at the beginning of this chapter. The only exception is the Half Rosettes. They are easiest to construct with the row method. The directions for basic row construction can be found at the start of the Hexagons chapter.

▼ Rosette—This is a simple ring motif.

▼ Left Corner Rosette—Extra pieces are added to the sides of the basic rosette to make the hexagon border and turn the corner.

▼ Right Corner Rosette—The mirror image of the left corner.

▼ Irregular Edge Rosette—Extra pieces are added to the sides of the basic rosette to make the hexagon border.

▼ Straight Edge Rosette—Used to complete the straight edge of the quilt and includes the hexagon border.

▼ Half Rosette—Used to complete the straight edge of the quilt and includes the hexagon border. I suggest this motif be constructed using row method rather than the motif method. Note the one-third hexagons that begin and end the first row. To be totally correct, this piece should be one-sixth of a hexagon, a piece that is difficult to cut. It is easier to use the one-third hexagon and trim it to match the straight edge prior to binding the quilt.

3. Construct the correct number of each motif. Refer to the chart, *Rosettes with Hexagon Border* Information, at the end of this section, for the required number of motifs.

4. Using row construction, join the motifs to make the quilt top.

5. Mark the quilting design on the quilt top. I suggest a continuous curve design. It is impossible to show you every line of stitching for the entire quilt top, but I show a partial block. There are dozens of possible stitching sequences. I use a continuous design worked in rings like the motifs. Motifs like rosettes and stars all work in much the same way.

Begin on the inside of the center block of the motif and stitch around all six sides. This will bring you full circle.

Stitch out into the second ring of hexagons. This row I call the petal row because the quilting lines look like petals. The line is on the inside of the second row of hexagons and on either side of every seam between the hexagons in the second ring. Stitch around the ring till you reach where you started. Then stitch up the last seam between the hexagons to reach the outside of the ring. *Notice that this line doesn't go back to the center.*

There is one side of stitching left to be done. This will be picked up at the very end of the quilting line.

Stitch the outside of the second ring. This line just scallops around the hexagons. When you reach the beginning of this row, stitch in to the third ring of hexagons.

Do the petal row on the inside of the third row. This is the inside seam and the seam between the hexagons in this ring. Upon reaching the last seam, stitch out the seam to the outside of the ring,

but do not stitch back in to the ring. *Notice there are unquilted lines in the design.* That is correct. They will be completed at the end of the quilting line.

Stitch the outside of the third ring. This line will scallop around the hexagons. When you reach the beginning you can move out into another ring of hexagons, or stitch back into the center of the motif to complete the quilting line.

Each ring of hexagons is the same as the previous line. The first section of stitching is the petal row, the second the scallop row.

Marking the design is optional. It can be quilted freehand and unmarked by the experienced quilter.

6. Stitch the backing together and prepare the quilt for quilting. Layer and baste the quilt.

7. Quilt the quilt and finish with ½"-wide French bias binding.

Baby quilt layout

Rosettes with Hexagon Border Information

The quilt is offered in three sizes. The hexagon motifs require an odd number of rows to make the quilt edges balance. The odd rows limit the sizes available for the quilt.

	Crib	Twin	Double/Queen
Finished size	46" × 56"	70" × 104"	94" × 104"
Motif set	3 × 3	5 × 6	7 × 6
Number of motifs			
Rosette	2	14	23
Left Corner Rosette	2	2	2
Right Corner Rosette	2	2	2
Irregular Edge Rosette	2	8	8
Straight Edge Rosette	0	2	4
Half Rosette	2	4	6
Amount of fabric required (in yards)			
(The yardage for freezer paper cutting is in parentheses.)			
Rosette centers	1/8 (1/8)	1/4 (1/4)	1/2 (5/8)
First ring	1/3 (3/8)	1 (1 1/8)	1 3/8 (1 5/8)
Second ring	5/8 (3/4)	1 3/8 (1 5/8)	2 5/8 (3)
Third ring and inside of border	1 3/8 (1 3/4)	3 7/8 (4 3/4)	4 7/8 (6 7/8)
Paths	1 1/4 (1 3/8)	3 1/2 (4)	3 3/4 (5)
Backing	3 1/4	6	9
Binding	3/4	1	1
Cutting Guide			
(Add 1/2" to strip width if doing freezer paper cutting.)			
Rosette centers, 2 1/2" strips	1	2	6
Total pieces rosette centers	8	28	75
First ring, 2 1/2" strips	4	13	18
Total pieces first ring	52	176	246
Second ring, 2 1/2" strips	8	19	36
Total pieces second ring	106	356	498
Third ring and inside of border, 2 1/2" strips	17	50	65
Total pieces third ring & inside of border	238	696	910
Paths, 2 1/2" strips	6	11	11
Total pieces paths	72	150	154
Path half hexagons, piece A1, 2 1/2" strips	6	26	36
Total pieces path half hexagons	124	624	854
Path third hexagons, piece A2, 1 3/4" strips	4	12	17
Total pieces path third hexagons	56	184	258
Border half piece (matches the third ring), piece A1, 2 1/2" strips	1	2	2
Total pieces border half piece	16	36	44

Twin quilt layout

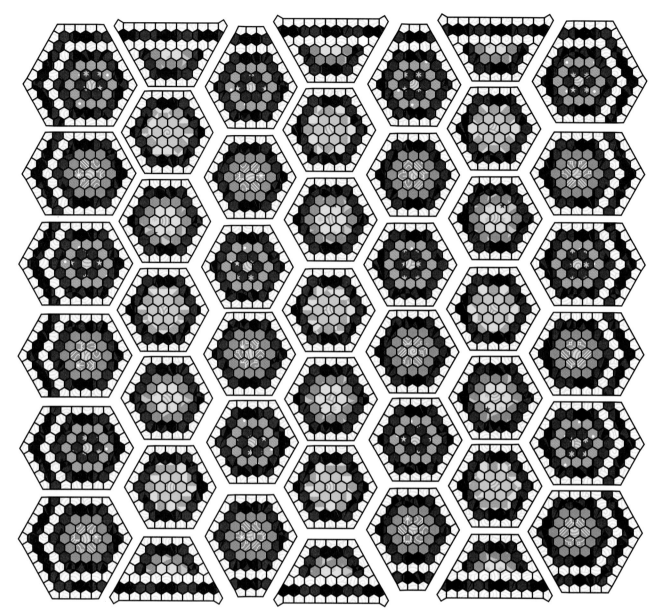

Double/Queen quilt layout

Stars and Rosettes

The *Stars and Rosettes* is my favorite hexagon pattern. It is a very old pattern and has many variations. Like the previous rosette pattern, the stars need to be divided into large hexagons to simplify joining the motifs. I chose to have the star as the center of the motif and divided the rosettes to make the large hexagons. The stars and rosettes are made from an assortment of print fabrics. The yardage is given for each ring to help you plan your own version of this pattern. The large scale of the design is not suitable for irregular edges. The quilt has straight edges and is finished with a border. The pattern is offered in one size — 83" × 93".

BLOCK SIZE

The basic star motif measures 21" × 24½"

Pieces and corresponding strip sizes

Piece A, hexagon: 2½" strip—yields 14 pieces
Piece A1, half hexagon: 2½" strip—yields 24 pieces
Piece A2, third hexagon: 1¾" strip—yields 16 pieces

PIECING DIRECTIONS

1. Cut the required number of pieces from each of the fabrics. Refer to the chart, *Stars and Rosettes* Information, at the end of this section, for the required number of pieces in each color. The pieces may be cut and marked in any method you choose. Mark all the matching dots on every piece. I recommend rotary cutting with the freezer paper cutting and stitch marking explained in the Freezer Paper Lesson in the *Quintettes* section of this chapter.

2. There are six basic motifs to this pattern:

▼ Star—This ring motif is based on the star and part of six rosettes.

▼ Left Corner Star— The basic star motif modified by adding and removing pieces to make a square corner.

▼ Right Corner Star—The mirror image of the left corner.

▼ Irregular Edge Star—The basic star motif modified by removing six pieces to make a straight edge.

▼ Straight Edge Triangle— A thirteen piece triangle that completes the rosettes along the irregular edge.

▼ Half Star—Used to complete the straight edge of the quilt and includes the hexagon border.

3. Begin by piecing the basic star motif. The star is based on a two ring rosette. Construct the rosette following the basic instructions at the start of the section, Hexagon Motif-Based Patterns.

4. The star is easiest to piece following the design rather than in rings. It is much like the dia-

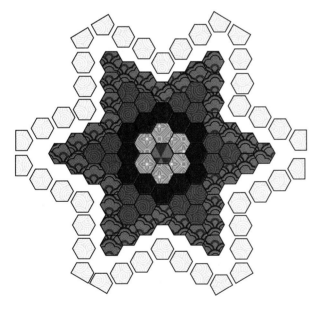

mond. Extra pieces are added to the rosette to make the shape of the star. Join the pieces that make the inside points of the stars. These will not make a complete ring.

5. Join the Star edge. This row will form a complete ring that is in the shape of a star.

6. To complete the star motif, join the hexagons for the rosettes. The next row is the third ring of the rosette. It will make a full ring and is the first row that has partial hexagons.

The next row is the second row of the rosette. It is added to the six sides of the sides and will not make complete rings.

The next row is the first row of the rosette. It is added to the six sides of the sides and will not make complete rings.

The last row adds the corner pieces that are the rosette centers. This piece is made from a one-third hexagon.

7. To piece the Straight Edge Triangle, use the motif method of construction. There are not many pieces to this triangle. Start piecing with the rosette center.

8. To piece the Half Star, use the motif method of construction. The motif method is the easiest when working with this complex pattern and colors. The only change in the basic method will be in the number of pieces in a ring. Instead of full rings the half motif is made of half rings. Start with the star center, just as you did in the basic star motif in step 3.

9. Construct the correct number of each motif. Refer to the chart, *Stars and Rosettes* Information, that follows, for the required number of motifs.

10. Using row construction, join the motifs to make the quilt top.

11. The hexagon blocks on the four quilt edges must be cut to make the quilt edge straight. On the two long sides the quilt edge is equal to the edges of the hexagons. Line up the ruler with the edges of the hexagons to locate the straight edge. On the top and bottom, the quilt edge will be in the middle of the hexagons. Remember to add ¼" for the seam allowance. Straighten the quilt.

12. Cut the borders from the required yardage. Cut four strips 10" × 94". The four border strips will be the measure of the longest side plus 1". The border can have butted or mitered corners.

13. Mark the quilting design on the quilt top. Use the same basic continuous curve directions as for *Rosettes with Hexagon Border* (beginning with step 5 in that section).

14. Stitch the backing together and prepare the quilt for quilting. Layer and baste the quilt.

15. Quilt the quilt and finish with ½"-wide French bias binding.

Stars and Rosettes Information

Finished size	83" × 93"
Border size	10"
Motif set	3 × 3
Number of motifs:	
Star	2
Left Corner Star	2
Right Corner Star	2
Irregular Edge Star	2
Straight Edge Triangle	4
Half Star	2

Amount of fabric required (in yards)

(The yardage for freezer paper cutting is in parentheses.)

Star centers	1/8 (1/8)
First star ring	1/3 (3/8)
Second star ring	2/3 (5/8)
Inside the star points	1 (1 1/8)
Star edge	1 1/3 (1 5/8)
Rosette center	1/4 (1/3)
First rosette ring	2/3 (3/4)
Second rosette ring	1 1/3 (1 5/8)
Third rosette ring	2 (2 3/8)
Backing	5 1/2
Binding	7/8

Cutting Guide

(Add 1/2" to strip width if doing freezer paper cutting.)

Star centers, piece A, 2 1/2" strips	1
Total pieces star centers	10
First star ring, piece A, 2 1/2" strips	4
Total first star ring pieces	56
Second star ring, piece A, 2 1/2" strips	8
Total second star ring pieces	110
Inside the star points, piece A, 2 1/2" strips	12
Total inside the star points pieces	162
Star edge, piece A, 2 1/2" strips	18
Total star edge pieces	234
Rosette center, piece A1, 2 1/2" strips	1
Total rosette center pieces	8
Rosette center, piece A2, 1 3/4" strips	3
Total rosette center pieces	42
First rosette ring, piece A, 2 1/2" strips	5
Total first rosette ring pieces	70
First rosette ring, piece A1, 2 1/2" strips	4
Total first rosette ring pieces	92
Second rosette ring, piece A, 2 1/2" strips	14
Total second rosette ring pieces	186
Second rosette ring, piece A1, 2 1/2" strips	4
Total second rosette ring pieces	92
Third rosette ring, piece A, 2 1/2" strips	22
Total third rosette ring A pieces	300
Third rosette ring, piece A1, 2 1/2" strips	5
Total third rosette ring A1 pieces	100

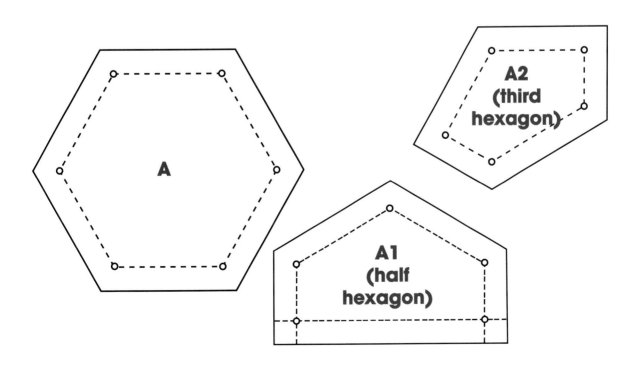

A

A2 (third hexagon)

A1 (half hexagon)

PART II

MACHINE QUILTING

Chapter 6

MACHINE QUILTING UPDATE

As any seasoned machine quilter will tell you, there is a lot more to machine quilting than putting the fabric under the presser foot. Many subtle skills are needed to be a master quilter. In fine-tuning skills, the practiced machine quilter needs to go beyond the beginner stage. That is what this chapter is about: the next steps beyond basics; the nitty-gritty steps between a good idea and how to make that idea really work. The accomplished quilter will find the answers to some of the more common machine quilting problems. For new machine quilters, these steps will give you an in-depth understanding of the nuances of machine quiltmaking.

Grid Quilting

Channel and grid quilting are a form of machine-guided quilting. They use the walking foot and feed dogs to move the fabric and make perfectly straight lines of identical stitches. The space between the lines of stitching can vary from under an inch to many inches apart. Channel quilting is parallel lines of stitching. Grid quilting is two sets of channel quilting running in opposite directions. The lines of stitching cross at 90 degrees, or 60 degrees, and cover the quilt with a checkerboard of stitching. Logically this should be the easiest type of quilting to do by machine. The machine is doing all of the work. The quilter simply follows the lines. Ah! *The lines!* Unless the channel or grid follows a pieced pattern or the quilt is made of plaid, the quilt maker has to mark the pattern.

Surprisingly little is written on how to successfully and quickly lay out channel or grid patterns for the machine quilter. Perhaps this lack of directions is because it seems so easy. It is merely straight lines. Anyone who has tried to mark a channel or grid pattern knows better. Many things can go wrong. The lines are long—for example, on a queen size quilt the diagonal can measure almost 12 feet. Such long lines are difficult to measure and keep even. They have to be an equal distance apart and all at the same angle. Plus, the grid lines have to make uniform squares. Added to that, the lines should match the corners of the quilt and every corner should form the same style of miter. What started as an easy design rapidly turns into a mathematical and logistical nightmare.

Unless, of course, you know the secrets to marking grid patterns.

Before laying out the grid, it is important to know a little about machine quilting grids. Thanks to Ernest B. Haight, machine quiltmakers have a wonderful way to do grid quilting I call ricochet quilting. The grid is laid out so the lines of stitching cross exactly on the quilt edge.

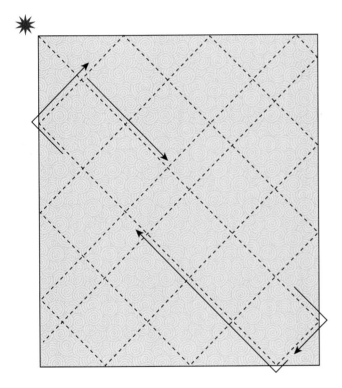

The illustration shows how a typical line of grid quilting is done on a quilt body. Note how the quilting lines form a 90-degree angle on the edge of the quilt body. The dotted lines show the stitching sequence. Start at the star and follow the line clockwise around the quilt. At the edge of the quilt stop with the needle lowered in the fabric. Lift the presser foot, pivot the fabric 90 degrees and continue. It's painless, fast, and simple. This way the quilting is done is long, unbroken lines of stitching. The method has a number of advantages. Laying out the grid in this manner looks great — so neat and accurate. The long lines of stitching mean less knots and a stronger quilting stitch. The lines of stitching are easy to stitch, and the quarter turns keep the majority of the quilt to the left of the needle. Most impor-

tant, the constant turning of the quilt changes the stitching directions. The frequent changes in direction result in a smoother, flatter quilt with less chance of puckers.

The key to the method is laying out the grid. This bit of logic, laying out the grid to make 90-degree corners at the edges of the quilt is a stroke of genius. When you know how the edges of the quilt are marked, it is a simple matter to connect the marks on the edges to form the grid, or channel, or any of the other straight line variations. The whole process is relatively easy. The results are awesome: the angles are always perfect, the lines always parallel and even, the corners lines all miter, and everything looks well planned.

There is one constant to this method of quilting. The grid must be on the diagonal to the straight edges of the quilt. The lines aren't limited to a 90-degree angle, but the method won't work if the grid is parallel or perpendicular to the edges.

My best words of advice are, "Relax and learn to cheat!" Grid quilting only appears perfect. It is never as perfectly measured as it looks. There are so many lines that the viewer sees the whole. Small errors and *even* medium size errors are easy to conceal.

The following samples demonstrate how to lay out grid designs. The same basic layout can be used to make a number of variations on grid quilting, including channel quilting, Hanging Diamonds, and other straight line designs.

Ninety-Degree Grid in the Body of the Quilt

This method of grid quilting is frequently seen on Amish quilts. The body of the quilt is done in a grid, while the borders have motif quilting. To give you a better understanding of the process, the sample numbers will be for a full-size quilt. The illustrations are simplified and exaggerated to make the directions clearer. The size of the quilt body for the sample is 53" × 70". I have chosen to use a 1½" grid.

1. The first step is to determine the distance between the lines of the grid. The parallel lines of the grid are 1½" apart. Because the grid is on an angle to the quilt edges, you need to know the distance between the grid lines when measured at a 45-degree angle. The 45-degree measurement is called the diagonal measure of the grid. Don't worry, this doesn't require math. I did all the math for you for the common sizes of grid and have listed them in a chart in the Appendix. In this example, the diagonal measure for 1½" grid is 2⅛". You will use 2⅛" to mark the quilt. Marking 2⅛" along the quilt edges will result in 1½" grid quilting.

2. Mark the repeats along the shortest edges of the quilt body. Start measuring at the exact corner (or the exact corner of the seamlines of the binding). Don't try to draw any lines at this point. Simply use a ruler and mark dots, 2⅛" apart along the short edge of the quilt body.

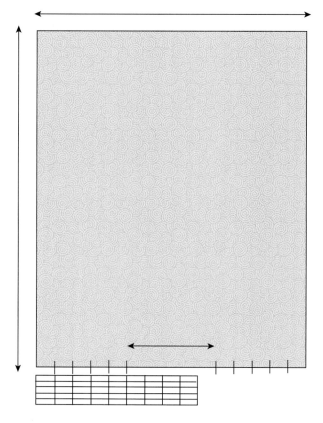

Don't measure 2⅛", move the ruler, and measure another 2⅛", and so on across the quilt. Every time you move the ruler there is a chance for errors.

Rather than measuring each division 2⅛" at a time, use the Repeats Guide in the Appendix. Listed below are the repeats up to 19⅛".

2⅛"	1 space
4¼"	2 spaces
6⅜"	3 spaces
8½"	4 spaces
10⅝"	5 spaces
12¾"	6 spaces
14⅞"	7 spaces
17"	8 spaces
19⅛"	9 spaces

I make a mark on the ruler at each repeat of 2⅛". I use a Vis á Vis water-based pen to mark on the plastic, then cover the marks with transparent tape. To remove the marks, peel off the tape and wipe the ruler with a damp cloth. The ruler in the illustration is marked according to the divisions. For even easier marking, use one of the many adhesive paper labels used to mark file folders. These labels are available from office supply stores.

Place the ruler along the quilt edge, with zero at the exact corner (or the exact corner of the seamlines of the binding). Make a mark at 2⅛", then 4¼", then every 2⅛" across to 19⅛". Move the ruler to the other corner of the quilt body and repeat the steps. There should be about a 15" unmarked section in the center of the edge. On the average, I leave a large space, 15" to 24" unmarked in the center. The larger the center space, the easier it is to make any adjustments in the pattern. The spaces in the center will be reduced or enlarged slightly to make the repeats fit the edge. I have *never* had the repeats work out perfectly. There is always some fitting to make the repeats fit. Don't panic. This doesn't require math on small grids.

I have three examples to explain how to fit the repeats to the space.

The Perfect Fit

When I measure the distance between the last mark on the right side of center and the last mark on the left side of center, the distance between them is 14⅞". Referring to the Repeat Guide, I see the measurement is perfect for 7 spaces. I can use the measuring guide and mark the 2⅛" spaces.

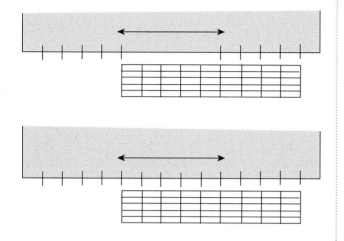

The Space is Too Short

When I measure the distance between the last mark on the right side of center and the last mark on the left side of center, the distance between them is 14". Referring to the Repeat Guide, I see the closest space should measure 14⅞". I am about 1" too short for the seven spaces. To correct the error, each space will have to be about ⅛" narrower. At this point you could do some basic math to fit the repeats to the space. I prefer a more visual method; I space the repeats by "eye." Simply slide the ruler to fit the repeats to the spaces. Start by sliding the ruler about ⅛" to the right and mark the first mark on the right side. Slide the ruler another ⅛" to the right and mark the second mark. Slide the ruler another ⅛" to the right and mark the next mark. Notice with each ⅛" move of the ruler, the beginning of the ruler is getting closer to the last dot on the left side of center. Continue to slide the ruler and mark the spaces until the ruler beginning is on the last dot on the left. Then mark the rest of the spaces without moving the ruler.

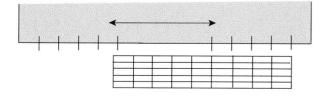

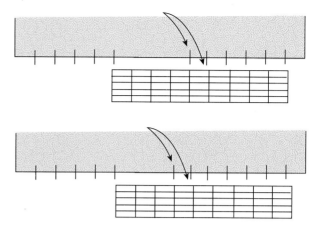

The Space is Too Long

When I measure the distance between the last mark on the right side of center and the last mark on the left side of center, the distance between them is slightly under 16". Referring to the measuring guide, I see the closest space should measure 14⅞". I am about 1" too long for the seven spaces. To correct the error, each space will have to be about ⅛" wider. At this point you could do some basic math to fit the repeats to the space. An easier solution is to slide the ruler to fit the repeats to the spaces. Start by sliding the ruler about ⅛" to the left and mark the first mark. Slide the ruler another ⅛" to the left and mark the second mark. Slide the ruler another ⅛" to the left and mark the next mark. Notice with each ⅛" move of the ruler, the beginning of the ruler is getting closer to the last dot on the left side of center. Continue to slide the ruler and mark the spaces until the beginning of the ruler is on the last dot on the left. Then mark the rest of the spaces without moving the ruler.

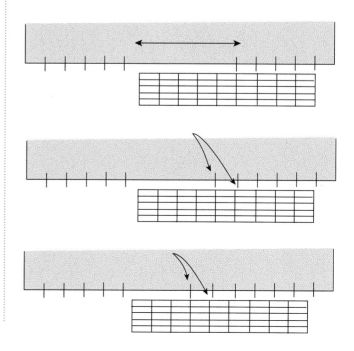

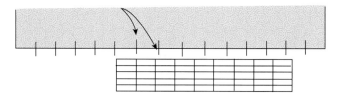

3. Mark the repeats along the longest edges of the quilt body, following the basic instruction in step 2.

4. Lay the quilt top on a large flat surface—a table top or on an uncarpeted floor. Mark the grid. Using a 24" rotary ruler start marking the grid in a corner of the quilt body. Join the first two dots on either edge with a straight line.

Continue marking, working toward the middle of the quilt. As the length of the line becomes longer, it is easier if you mark the quilt top with a friend or mate helping to move and hold the ruler. The 24" ruler will become too short for the length of the grid line. Change to a longer straight edge. Be creative; any long straight edge will work.

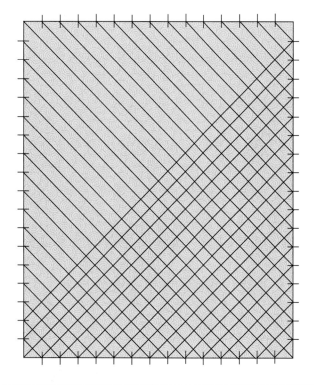

MARKING LESSON
What Can Go Wrong and How to Cheat: In the previous steps I explained how to perfectly fit the repeats to the space. In the sample it worked out wonderfully. But things can go wrong. The larger the space between the grid, the more likely it is you will have to do some simple math. Look back at the first sample. Divide the length and width by the diagonal number (2⅛") to determine the number of repeats per side.

$$53 \div 2.125" = 24.94$$
$$70 \div 2.125" = 32.94$$

Each of the measures is only .06 or 1/16 off from a whole repeat. That's almost perfect. (For a decimal equivalent chart, see the Appendix).

Dividing the width and length by the diagonal number may result in a larger fraction, like 23¼" repeats or 35¾" repeats. For example 71" divided by 2⅛" equals 33.41 repeats. This is where cheating on the measurements of the repeats is required. On small diagonal measurements like the 2⅛", any fraction of a repeat is so small, it is easy to divide it among the few spaces in the center. The smaller the grid the easier it is to lay out.

As the grid becomes larger, it is harder to mark the quilt without doing math. For example, 71" divided by 5⅝" equals 12.62 or about 12½ repeats. When each repeat measures 5⅝", half a repeat is almost 3". That amount is more difficult to divide between a few spaces in the center of the quilt. There is only one solution. Divide the partial repeat among all the spaces. Round the decimal number of repeats to the closest whole number. 12.62 would round up to 13 repeats. Divide the length of the side (71") by the number of repeats (13). That equals 5.46 or approximately 5½" instead of 5⅝". The measurement of the repeat on the 71" side is now 5½". Repeat the steps for the other side of the quilt. The measurements of the repeats may not be exactly the same on short and long edges of the quilt. Don't worry: the grid will still be uniform and the slight discrepancy will never show.

MARKING HINT
Marking Long Straight Lines: Long straight lines are hard to mark unless you have a long straight edge. I use an acrylic bar. The bar is extruded in the shape of an Equilateral Triangle. It measures 1" on each edge. It is lightweight and strong and stable. I own a number of lengths: 6', 10', and 12'. The acrylic bar is purchased by the foot from plastic suppliers or lumber yards. I obtained mine from Plastics to Go in Minneapolis, Minnesota, at a cost of about $1.25 a foot. Storage can be a problem with long rulers. I store mine along the baseboard on my sewing room floor.

5. Mark from corner to corner in one direction. Then mark the grid in the other direction.

Grid Variations

In the previous examples the grid forms a miter in the corner of the quilt. The marking is started at the exact corner. Another way to mark the top is to measure in a half repeat and make the first mark at that point. This results in a squared corner with a line of stitching on either side of the true corner. This method of marking is extremely successful for border grids and makes the borders easier to stitch.

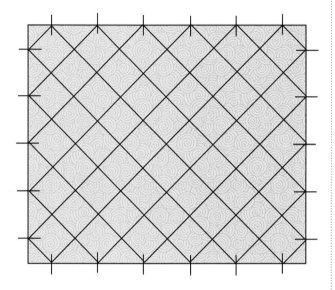

Not all grids are based on the 90-degree angle. A variation of grid is called Hanging Diamonds. This grid is based on a 60-degree angle. Look at the illustration.

The grid is narrow and long. The spaces marked on the two edges are different measurements. The spaces on the long side are twice as big as the spaces on the short side. To make Hanging Diamonds, use the charts in the Appendix. Mark the shortest edge

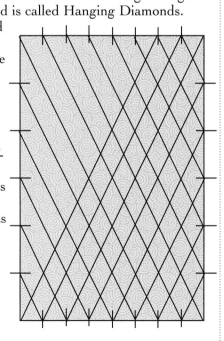

of the quilt body with the measurement for the smaller grid. Mark the long edge of the quilt body with the measurement for the larger grid. The Hanging Diamonds will happen automatically when you draw the grid. The ratios for Hanging Diamonds are:

Grid	On the Diagonal
½" to 1"	¾" to 1⅜"
1" to 2"	1⅜" to 2⅞"
1½" to 3"	2⅛" to 4¼"
2" to 4"	2⅞" to 5⅝"

This method of measuring the edge first will also work for channel and other straight line designs. For more design ideas, I recommend *Quilting with Style, Principles for Great Pattern Design* by Gwen Marston and Joe Cunningham.

Ninety-Degree Grid on Borders

The illustration shows how grid quilting is done on a border. Note how the grids intersect on the inside edge of the border. The heavy lines show the stitching sequence. Start at the star and follow the line clockwise around the border. When you reach the small arrow at the end of the first line, simply turn on the next line and continue around the quilt. Stitch row after row of lines, zigzagging around the border. It's painless, fast, and simple.

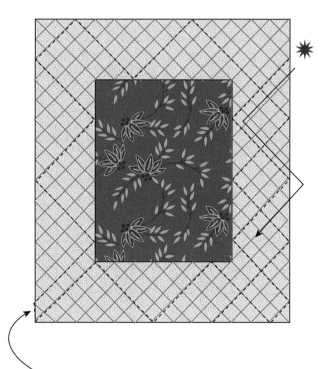

1. Measure the inside edges of the border. The outside dimensions are unimportant. For the sample I will use the same quilt I used in the previous example. The inside edges of the border measure 53" × 70". The grid is 1½".

2. Mark the quilt using steps 1 through 4 from the earlier section, Ninety-Degree Grid in the Body of the Quilt.

3. Lay the quilt top on a large flat surface—a table top or on an uncarpeted floor. Mark the grid. In the previous example the grid was marked on the quilt body. To mark the borders, draw the grid on the borders. It is impossible to mark the borders without using a long straight edge like an acrylic bar. Using a long straight edge, start marking the grid in a corner of the quilt body. Line up the bar on the first two dots on either edge of the corner. Mark the straight lines into the border. Continue working toward the middle of the quilt. As the length of the line becomes longer, it is easier to mark the quilt top with the help of a friend or mate helping to move and hold the straight edge.

4. Mark from corner to corner in one direction. Then mark the grid in the other direction.

5. The outside corners of the borders will be marked last. Using a 24" ruler, line up the last mark in the corner with the 1½" mark on the ruler and draw in the first line of the outer corner. Mark the remaining lines in each corner to complete the design.

Continued on page 120

STITCHING LESSON

How to Stitch the Grid: A few tricks can make the grid easier to stitch. The illustration shows

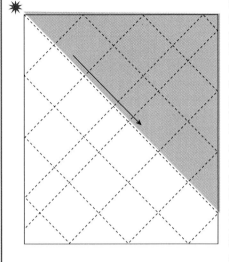

the grid on the inside of the quilt body. The shaded area shows what portion of the quilt will be to the right of the needle and under the head on the machine. Notice that it is about one-half of the quilt. It is important that no more than one-half of the quilt is to the right of the needle. The next illustration shows the last stitching line indicated on the original drawing. Even on this

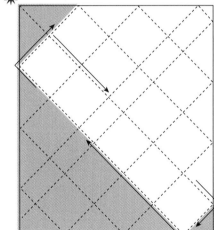

line there is only about one-half of the quilt to the right.

Watch what would happen if you were to continue stitching by pivoting counter-clockwise. The next line of quilt-

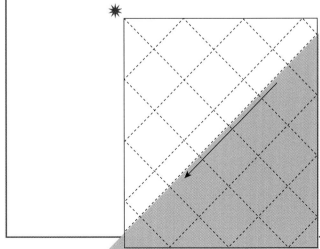

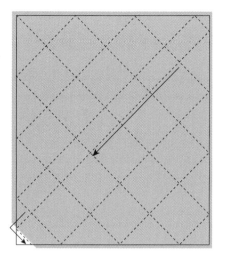

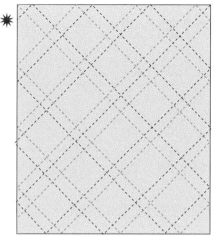

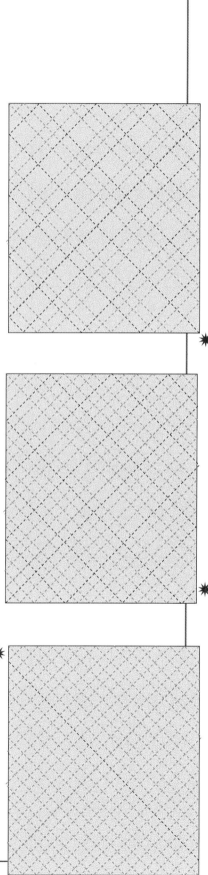

ing is a short line across the corner of the quilt. Notice that almost all of the quilt is to the right and under the machine head. It would be impossible to sew.

The best solution is to break the thread and begin a new line of quilting. There are a dozen alternatives, but for the sample, start again in the upper left hand corner and stitch a second line at a right angle to the first line. This line ends in the corner of the quilt. Break the thread and start a third line of stitching. This time start in the opposite corner and repeat the first two lines of stitching. There will be one line of quilting that will not be stitched using the four lines. Finish this line to complete the quilt top. This illustration is typical of stitching a grid for three reasons.

▼ It is important that the first line of stitching start at the left side of a short edge of the quilt.

▼ You must stop stitching when more than half of the quilt is under the head of the machine. Don't try to plan ahead. It is very obvious when you get to that point. You will know to stop stitching on this line and start another.

▼ Almost every quilt requires multiple lines of stitching. The best part is the lines are usually in pairs. Notice in the sample that two lines started in the upper left corner and two identical lines started in the opposite corner. There may be one pair of lines, a line in each corner, or a half dozen pairs of lines, six starting from each corner. On some quilts the pairs start in all four corners. The best way to stitch is to start in a corner and work until you can stitch no farther. Than turn the quilt and stitch the matching line in the opposite corner.

There are no magic formulas for stitching the grid. Every quilt is different. The height and width change the stitching sequence. The best news is the process is simple and obvious. After a line or two of stitching you will begin to see the pattern and be able to continue in a logical way.

Notice in the illustration that the lines of stitching on the outside edge of the quilt do not meet to form 90-degree angles. That is a common occurrence. The only way to make the lines of stitching meet perfectly on both edges of the border is to mathematically design the width of the border. To work out perfectly, the border width must be evenly divisible by the size of the repeat. Rather than doing math and cutting the quilt to match the design, simply ignore the less-than-perfect outer edge. Skip from one line to another along the edge. The outside will be covered with binding and will be concealed.

6. A border of Hanging Diamonds can marked in the same method.

New and Improved Quilt-As-You-Go

The idea of Quilt-As-You-Go is tantalizing. The most difficult part of machine quilting is handling the bulk of the quilt. Trying to fit a queen-size quilt in the small space of the sewing machine is a nightmare. It would be so much easier to handle if the body of the quilt could be completed in sections, then the sections combined to make the quilt. To be honest, I hate the old Quilt-As-You-Go methods. The methods limited the piecing and quilting pattern. They don't work for quilts like *Lone Star*, *Amish Bars*, or medallion-style quilts, plus they require hand stitching, the nemesis of machine quiltmakers. Nothing is more irksome than taking hours to hand stitch the backing of a machine-made quilt.

One method of Quilt-As-You-Go solves all the problems. It doesn't limit the design of the quilt or quilting pattern. It doesn't have any hand stitching, and it makes the quilt in sections. It is based on a block construction method developed by Emiko Toda Loeb of New York, NY. Ms Loeb is famous for her reversible *Log Cabin* quilts. It is similar to an older method of quilting called "stitch and flip." The method is applicable to almost any style of quilt.

The basic premise is the middle of the quilt is the hardest to quilt. And no matter how large the quilt, the borders are always the easiest to stitch. Anything within 24" of the edge is simple to fit under the arm of the machine. That translates to a 48" square, 24" inches in from each edge, as the largest piece that can be comfortably handled. The secret is to keep the distance from the quilt edges to the center of the quilt sections under the magic 24" mark.

Basic Instructions

This method requires a simple seaming method. All the variations are based on this seam.

1. Section A represents a quilted portion of the quilt. It could be a single block or a strip of blocks, sashing, or a section as large as the center of a *Lone Star* quilt. The section has been pieced and quilted. Notice the quilting can run off the edge of the fabrics.

2. Section B is the next section to be added to section A. It is unquilted at this step. The materials for Section B are the quilt top, quilt back,

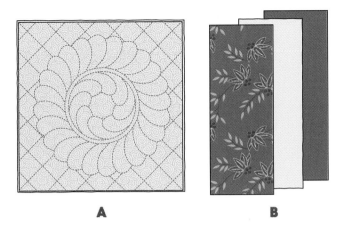

A   B

and batting. All the pieces are cut the size of the finished section plus the ¼" seam allowance on all edges.

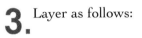

3. Layer as follows:

▼ Place the unquilted back of section B right side up.

▼ Stack Section A on top with the back down.

▼ Place the unquilted top of section B right side down on top of section A.

The two backs are right sides together. The two tops are right sides together.

4. Line up the edges and seam the layers together with a ¼" seam allowance. Stitch with the backing side up.

This seam is joining quilted layers to unquilted fabric. There are a number of factors that will affect this seam. High-loft batting or heavy quilting can cause the quilted section A to shrink slightly. The B piece should be cut to the *unquilted* measurement of piece A. It is common that the Bs will appear longer than the quilted As. That is to be expected. It is important that the quilt *top* B be eased to fit section A. Without easing the quilt can become misshapen.

Without easing, piece B will shrink during quilting and become smaller than piece A. With the addition of two or three more pieces, the outside of the quilt will be too small for the quilt interior and the quilt will not hang straight or lie flat.

The quilt backing is not as important. Usually the backing is stretched during the basting process. Sewing backing side up takes advantage of the machine's characteristic of easing the layer closest to the feed dogs while stretching the topmost layer.

5. Butt the batting to the edge of the batting in the seam.

6. Join the batting using the widest and longest zig-zag on your machine. The seam isn't very strong but it will hold the batting together until the quilting is in place.

7. Tip the quilt top and back over the batting, smoothing the seams. Pin baste the new section and quilt it.

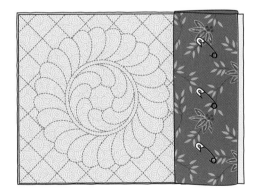

8. After the quilting is complete, trim away any excess batting extending beyond the edges of the section.

9. Section B is ready to be joined to the next section.

The following examples demonstrate a number of ways to use this method.

Strip Quilting

The strip method of quilting is applicable to a number of quilt sets, both straight and diagonal. It can be used to join strips of blocks to sashing or adjoining rows of blocks. Other applications include *Strippy* quilts or *Amish Bar* quilts.

The quilt in the illustration is a simple block and sashing.

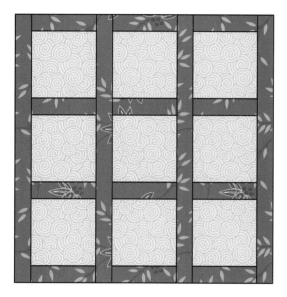

1. Join three blocks with the sashing strips to make the center strip. Layer and quilt this strip.

2. Trim any extra batting from around the quilt body.

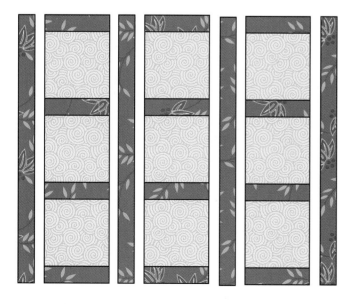

3. Add the next strip (the sashing) to the right side of the center, following the basic seaming instructions explained earlier in this section.

4. Quilt the second strip.

5. Add the third strip to the left side of the center and quilt.

6. Continue to add strips on alternating sides of the center.

Unit Quilting

The unit method is primarily used on large-scale designs like Amish pattern or medallion-style quilts. The method is combined with the border quilting to make the complete quilt. The quilt in this sample is an Amish *Square in Square* pattern.

1. Begin with the center square of the *Square in Square* block. Layer and quilt this section.

2. Add the triangle on one side of the square following the basic seaming instructions. Quilt the triangle.

3. Add the remaining triangles, one at a time, following the basic seaming instructions. Quilt the triangles.

4. Add the borders.

Border Construction

The border method is applicable for single or multiple borders. It is the last step to completing

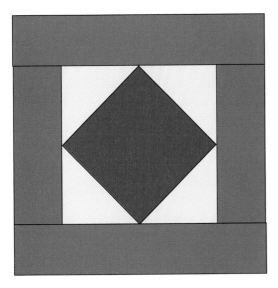

the quilt. The quilt in this sample is the Amish design constructed in the previous steps.

1. Construct and quilt the quilt body.

2. Trim any extra batting from around the quilt body.

3. The border can be butted corners or mitered.

Butted Corners

Butted corner borders are done in exactly the same sets as usual borders, with the exception of using the Quilt-As-You-Go seam in place of traditional seaming. Add a border to opposite sides of

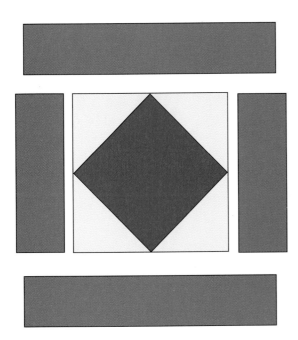

the quilt body, and quilt the borders. Then complete the quilt by adding the remaining two borders.

Mitered Corners

Mitered corners with the Quilt-As-You-Go method are not for the timid. They are not hard, but are inherently more complex because mitered corners are more difficult than butted corners. The basic steps for a mitered corner are the same as they are for a usual border see Adding Borders to the Quilt in the chapter, Quilter's Schoolhouse. As you might surmise, it is almost impossible to sew the front and back miter at the same time. It is better to treat the front and back borders as separate pieces, first joining the front border, then adding the back border. The key is to sew the top border to the quilt, mark and stitch the miters, than add the back border and make the mitered corners on the backing.

After the borders have been joined to the quilt and mitered, the batting is slipped between the borders. The batting could be mitered just like the borders, but it is easier to to work with if it is cut with butted corners, not mitered. I join the border batting to the short sides of the quilt first. The batting for the short sides is cut in a rectangle the width of the border by the width of the quilt body. Turn back the borders and join the batting to the quilt body (see steps 5 and 6 of the basic instructions earlier in this section). The batting for the long sides is cut in a rectangle the width of the border by the finished length of the quilt. Turn back the borders and join the batting to the quilt body and the batting from the short sides of the border.

Improving Your Machine-Guided Quilting Skills

This chapter is not written as a step-by-step lesson. Instead it contains short descriptions of techniques that will improve your machine guided quilting. Some of the problems covered in this chapter are:

▼ The backing pleats as it is quilted and the quilt looks flat in comparison to hand quilted quilts.

▼ Knotting the end of the lines of stitching is tedious.

▼ There are strange lines or creases between adjacent lines of straight quilting.

▼ There are pleats where stitching lines cross.

▼ The quilt isn't flat and doesn't hang straight.

The backing pleats as it is quilted, and the quilts look flat in comparison to hand-quilted quilts.

There is one solution to both of these problems: Stretch the backing taut before pinning the quilt. This step is extremely important. The backing should be stretched ½" to 1" for every 36" in width and length. For an example I will use a small baby quilt backing cut to measure 36" by 45". Stretching the backing ½" to 1" for 36" would result in a quilt back that measures approximately 36½" by 46" when stretched for the basting process. This step ensures a flat, uncreased backing, and guarantees a dimensional appearance on the front of the quilt. For even more dimension, do not prewash the fabric for the quilt backing. Do prewash the fabric for the quilt top. After the quilt is completed, wash the quilt in tepid water. The backing will shrink slightly and the top will become more raised.

Knotting the end of the lines of stitching is tedious.

Most quilters knot the beginning and end of the line of stitches by reducing the stitch length to a very short stitch length. This can be accomplished by a number of methods. On some machines the knot is programmed into the computer; on other machines the stitch length adjustment has to be made manually. Either way, the quilter has to adjust what the machine is doing. This constant changing of the settings on the machine, no matter how easy, becomes an aggravation. There is a way to make a knot without touching anything on the machine.

When you reach the spot you want to knot, press down on the quilt to hold it against the bed of the machine and stop it from feeding forward. The feed dogs and walking foot will try to move the fabric while you are resisting the motion. The result will be tiny stitches that will make a secure knot. By gently tugging on the quilt, you can pull the fabric towards you and make a few stitches going backwards. This makes a secure knot without touching the reverse button. I call this knot the *Hold Knot*. It doesn't hurt the sewing machine and it's so easy, it seems wrong.

There are strange lines or creases between adjacent lines of straight quilting.

Every machine-quiltmaker knows what this looks like. It happens on long straight lines of stitching like grid quilting or on sashing and is most likely to happen with high loft batting. This effect is called "sheering." It is caused by the grain lines shifting during the stitching. The grain shifts because the walking foot and feed dogs are not moving the fabric in perfect unison. The effect is exacerbated by the backing being stretched during the pinning process.

To practice the technique use an unstarched 12" square of striped or small checked fabric for the quilt top, or draw a 1" line across a plain fabric square. The lines, like the stripes, indicate the grainline and show what is going wrong. Use the striped fabric as the quilt top, layer it with batting and a backing 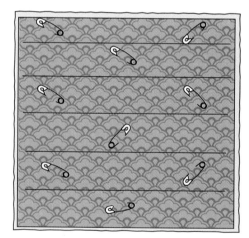 and pin baste it together. Use the regular zig-zag presser foot, not the walking foot.

Start sewing at the top edge, crossing the stripes, and sew to the lower edge. Pivot, lift the presser foot, and move over about 2" from the first line. Sew a second line from the lower edge to the top. Lift the presser foot, move about 2" and sew a third line from the top to the bottom. Now look closely at the grainlines. Notice how the grainline zig-zags between the quilting lines? The presser foot pushed the fabric ahead of the quilting line. When the quilting was stitched from the other direction, it forced the fabric in the opposite direc-

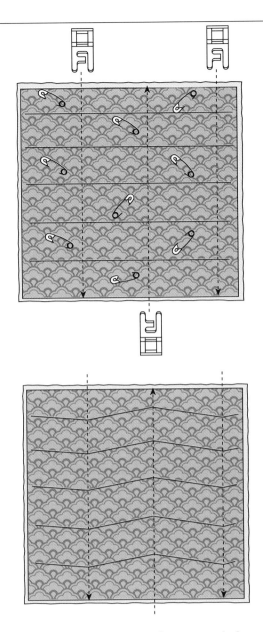

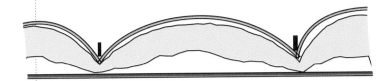

ric as you quilt. It is much the same skill used in easing sleeve caps to an armscye. You will use your fingertips to nudge a small amount of fabric under the presser foot. Use the walking foot for this sample.

1. Place your hands in front of the presser foot, fingertips together, elbows out. Your fingers should be about 2" in front of the foot.

2. Slide your fingers across the top layer of the quilt, toward the presser foot, until there is a small bubble between your fingers and the presser foot. Use a light touch. Don't move the batting or the backing, just the quilt top.

3. Start to sew and coax the fabric bubble under the foot. Use your fingertips to constantly help the top layer of fabric feed smoothly under the foot. These are subtle, small movements that become an automatic part of quilting.

Not sure you're doing it correctly? There is a way to determine your skill level.

Repeat steps 1 and 2. As you start to sew, *force* the bubble under the presser foot to make a pleat in the line of quilting. I know it looks wrong. *It is wrong!* It is not good machine quilting, but it is great practice. Learning to make a pleat teaches you how

tion. The grain line is trapped at an angle between the two lines of quilting. That angled grain line is called sheering.

The walking foot can correct some of this effect, but a presser foot cannot replace the sense of touch or sight. You have to become aware of the grain lines as you stitch and control how they are moving.

Look at a cross section of the quilt sandwich. During the pinning process the backing is stretched while the batting and quilt top are relaxed. After the pinning is complete, the backing is released and returns to its original size. This results in extra fabric and batting on the quilt top. The illustration shows an exaggerated effect. The odd arrangement of too much fabric on top for too little on the bottom, helps keep the backing smooth and flat. The extra top fabric makes the quilt look dimensional. The key to stitching the quilt is to ease the top fabit feels to control the fabric as you sew. Try to quilt a line of tiny pleats. Notice that the small pleats aren't really held by the stitches. A slight brush with your finger across the tiny pleat will make it disappear. Next quilt a line where the top layer is eased but doesn't have any pleats.

Now layer and pin baste another 12" of striped fabric, batting, and backing. Repeat the first three steps, this time nudging the fabric under the foot and using the walking foot. The grainlines will be straight and there will not be any sheering. Congratulations!

There are pleats where stitching lines cross.

This is caused by the presser foot pushing the top layer of fabric. It is the same effect as sheering and can be corrected in the same way. To solve the problem, be more aggressive in nudging the fabric under the presser foot. The place most quilters make the mistake is in the last ½" before crossing a previous line. The ½" mark is the point of no return. Any extra fabric has to be eased in *before* that last ½". If there is too much fabric at that point, it will make a pleat no matter what you do.

There is a temptation to stretch the quilt at the seam line to remove the pleat. Stretching will remove the pleat, especially on a bias grid, but don't stretch the quilt. The cardinal rule of machine-guided quilting is "How it is sewed is how it stays." Stretching the quilt and sewing across the stretched area will cause a bubble in the quilt, a dimple that always pops up where the quilting lines cross. It is the same effect as ripple stitching on stretch fabric. Ripple stitch is a novelty stitching or edging used on stretchy fabric. The fabric is stretched to the maximum and then stitched or serged with a tight zag-zag or satin stitch. When the stretched fabric is released the edge ruffles from the stitches. The effect is permanent. That is what's happening to the quilt when it is stretched and sewn. It stays stretched permanently.

The quilt isn't flat and doesn't hang straight.

The quilt top was flat and straight. The edges were even and the top square. Yet somewhere between the piecing and the quilting, everything got out of alignment. There may be bubbles or lumps in the quilt at the seamlines. The quilting lines might dimple, and the quilt is no longer square. There are solutions for these problems.

First, press open the seams. Open seams are less bulky than seams pressed to one side. The seam allowances on intricate piecing can be very thick. For hand quilters thick seam allowances are not a problem because hand quilting doesn't compact the quilt layers as machine quilting does. Not only do the thick seam allowances make a lump on the quilt top, they also make the quilt stiff where the quilting crosses the seam allowances.

Second, don't stretch the fabric as you quilt. Dimples on the quilt top are caused by stretching the quilt when it is sewn. It can be caused by the quiltmaker stretching the quilt as it is stitched. It can also happen when the presser foot gets "hung up" or caught on a heavy seam. Open seams will reduce the possibility of the catching on a thick seam.

An out-of-square or a buckled quilt is a more serious problem. Pressing open seams can help, as does proper feeding of the fabric on machine guided lines of stitching. More often the effect is caused by the choice of quilting pattern. Some patterns, especially heavily stitched fillers like grid or stipple quilting, pucker the quilt. The less quilted areas don't pucker as much and appear bowed or buckled. The quilt will lie flat, but hanging it is a mess. Choose patterns that evenly distribute the amount of quilting through the entire quilt top.

It is possible to correct some of the buckle or bowing on a finished quilt by washing it in tepid water. Spin it twice in the regular spin cycle. Remove the quilt from the washer and lay it flat on a large surface like the floor. (I use my living room floor. It is carpeted. I cover it with sheets to make a clean surface for the quilt.) Smooth the quilt, tugging and pulling where necessary to make the quilt lay flat. Measure the quilt as it lays on the floor. Make sure all the edges are straight, the corners true, and the quilt measures the same on both diagonals. Leave it to dry for 6 to 12 hours, undisturbed. If you're lucky, the quilt will be square and flat.

Improving Your Free-Motion Quilting Skills

The chapter is not written as a step-by-step lesson. Instead it contains short lessons and descriptions of techniques that will improve you free-motion quilting skills. Some of the topics covered in this chapter are:

▼ Ergonomical considerations

▼ Secure and neat knots

▼ Tiny bumps of thread on the back of the quilt

▼ Erratic stitches at the beginning of a line of stitching or in the middle of long lines of stitching

▼ Stitching feather motifs

Ergonomical considerations

It is important to sit correctly and hold the fabric in the right way to prevent health problems like carpel tunnel syndrome, neckache, or back pain.

To sit comfortably at the machine, use a good secretarial chair with adjustable back, seat, and height. You should sit up straight, feet on the floor. The back of your legs should not be "cut" by the edge of the chair; this can cause blood clots and painful leg cramps. The chair back should support your lower back and prevent you from slouching. Sitting up straight with your shoulders relaxed will improve your breathing. This prevents headaches and fatigue. The sewing machine should be directly in front of you, with the needle clearly in your line of sight. The machine should be on a high enough surface so you do not bend or slouch to see the needle or presser foot. There should be at least a 6" space in front of the machine for resting your arms. A common cause of back and shoulder pain is having your arms dangling off the edge of the table. (This has the glamorous name of "flying elbows!") The table or cabinet should be arranged to support your arms in line with the presser foot. Carpal tun-

nel syndrome is caused in part by constant bending of the wrists. Keeping the fingers, wrist, and elbows in a straight line is called the "neutral" position and is the least apt to cause injury.

Many of the health complaints voiced by quilters are caused by "repetitive motion injuries." The most frequent cause is constant and prolonged stretches of quilting. The best guard against injury is taking frequent breaks from quilting. Follow an exercise program that stresses aerobic and stretching movements. Most importantly, listen to your body. If you're experiencing muscle fatigue, pain, or loss of motor control, stop sewing. Relax, stretch, and do something else. If the symptoms continue, see your physician.

Secure and neat knots

Knotting seems to be the most troublesome area of machine quilting. The knots need to be secure without being too obvious. A great knot is made of five to ten tiny, almost infinitesimal stitches. The tiny stitches pierce the warp and weft threads of the fabrics and securely tie off the ends. The problems arise when the stitches fall in exactly the same spot. The illustration shows what happens when the needle stitches repeatedly in the same spot. The top and bobbin thread twist together in a long knot, called a "pig tail." The knot isn't caught in the fab-

ric; it is just laying on the back of the quilt. When you clip the thread tails, you cut off the knot. The quilting stitches can rip out.

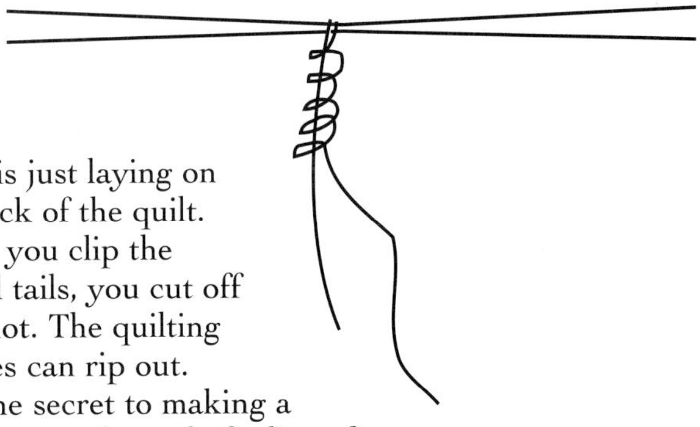

The secret to making a neat knot at the end of a line of stitching is in the way it is cut. First, cut the top thread tail close to the stitching. Then, flip the quilt to the back and tug on the bobbin thread tail. The tug pulls the small end of the top thread tail

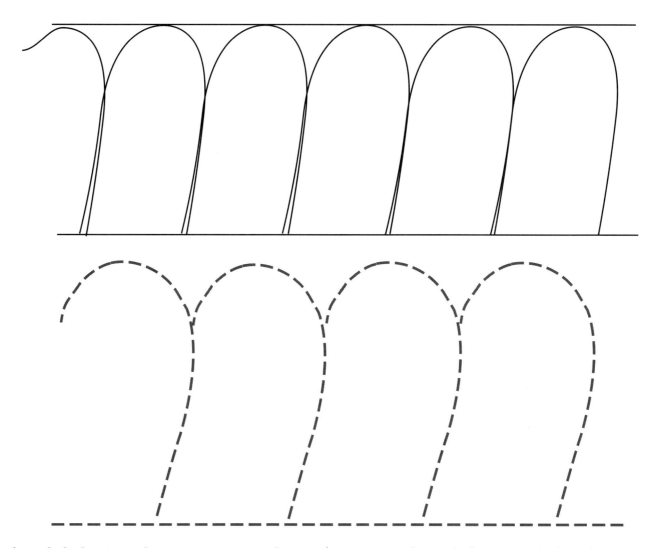

through the batting and removes any wisps of thread that can mar the quilt top. Cut off the bobbin thread tail to complete the knot.

At the beginning of a line of stitching, the bobbin thread is brought up through the quilt to ensure a neat start. This results in both the top and bobbin threads being on the quilt top. For a neat knot at the beginning of a line of stitching, tug both the top and bobbin threads and clip them close to the quilt top.

The stitches on the back of the quilt are tiny bumps of thread.

This is "pig tail" knots in the middle of the line of stitching. It is called "sand" or "sanding" because it looks like a line of sand along the bobbin side of the quilting line. There is only one cause for this effect. There are too many stitches too close together. Try to make longer stitches by sewing slower and moving your hands faster.

Erratic stitches at the beginning of a line of stitching or in the middle of long lines of stitching.

It common to have problems starting a line of stitches or resuming a line of stitching. For example, on a long line of stitching it is impossible to sew from one end to the other without having to move your hands. Usually you can machine quilt about 4" without losing control of the quilt. At this point you stop sewing with the needle lowered in the quilt, relocate your hands, and resume quilting. It's at this point, when you have just moved your hands and are restarting the machine, that one or two stitches make a zig. It's maddening!

The solution is simple. You are trying to do too many things at once: start the machine, pick up speed, move your hands and follow a line. It's akin to patting your head, rubbing your stomach, and riding a bicycle all at once. It's possible…but difficult. Just slow down. Don't do so much at a time. First, start the machine running slowly. Don't move your hands until you have taken a stitch or two. Then move your hands slowly as you pick up the machine speed. That's all there is to it.

Don't take more than a stitch or two before moving the fabric. Anymore stitches will result in a "pig tail" knot and sanding along the quilting line.

Stitching feather motifs

Feather motifs are the easiest to stitch using the M & M stitching sequence.

To practice feathers, draw two straight lines two inches apart and the feathered heart on a plain 12" square of muslin. Layer the muslin, batting, and backing and pin baste.

The best place to learn to stitch feathers is with a straight line of feathers. The illustration shows the similarities between the letter M and the shape of a traditional feather motif. Stitching long lines of the letter M is excellent practice. The letter M teaches the feel of stitching feathers, without the anxiety of following a pattern line. The M & M stitching sequence works with an existing skill, writing, to make it easy to learn to stitch feathers. The two straight lines are the base and top line for the feathers. Treat the lines as the lines on a sheet of paper. You will be writing the letter M between the lines. The lines will act as a guide for the height of the letter in much the same way as the lined paper guides a child learning to write. Start stitching at the left end of the lower straight line. "Write" a continuous M with the stitching line, like the illustration. The M is *not* drawn on the fabric, just sewn.

Don't worry about the uniformity of the letter; concentrate on developing a feel for the shape. Determine where is the best place to stop stitching when you need to relocate your hands (usually on the double line of stitching between the curves). Try to place the doubled lines of stitching directly on top of one another, and make smooth curves. In general, pay more attention to the stitch quality than to the uniformity of the pattern. It is easiest to learn a new skill if you break it down into small parts. In that way you're learning one thing at a time. With the M & M stitching you focus on stitch quality. The heart pattern will focus on following a pattern.

Improving your feather skills by stitching the Feathered Heart design (page 130). For this sample, always have the point of the heart pointed at you as you sew. Do not rotate the fabric.

1. Start stitching the heart at the star.

2. First stitch the feather vein. Stitch in a clockwise direction around the heart on the heavy dotted and dashed line. The line is easy to stitch and see as you move along the righthand side. On the lefthand side the line becomes more difficult to see and at about 9 o'clock the line is completely obscured by the foot.

In most designs there comes a place where the presser foot covers the design line. It is impossible to see where to stitch. This usually happens when the fabric is being pulled toward you in a diagonal direction. The design lines are under and in back of the foot. Of course you can turn the fabric to see more clearly, but often the quilt is too large to rotate a sufficient amount. The way to stitch this line is to look at the surrounding pattern. The vein is in the center of the feathers. The edges of the feathers are clearly visible, so guide the stitching by the feathers. Don't try to look into the presser foot opening to see the vein. Trust yourself to judge accurately the location of the vein.

3. When you reach the star, sew out on the lines of the feathers and begin doing the feathers on the right side of the heart. Work in a clockwise direction. When you reach the bottom of the heart, stitch along the vein to the bottom loop. Make the loop and stop stitching.

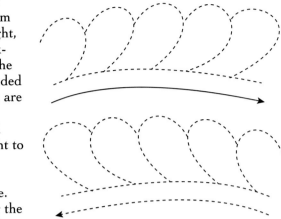

feathers? Look at the illustrations. Compare the two sets of feathers. The right-handed feathers are easiest to stitch from left to right, or clockwise. The left-handed feathers are best stitched from right to left, or counter clockwise. Stitching the feathers in the correct direction makes the longest, smoothest line of stitching.

Make a knot along the vein of the feather and break the thread. Move to the top of the feather and start again, stitching counter-clockwise.

4. Notice the feathers on the lefthand side of the heart are mirror images of the feathers on the righthand side of the heart.

Did you know there are right-and left-handed

5. Knot off the thread when you reach the end of the design.

6. Move to the inside feathers of the heart. Stitch these feathers to complete the motif.

Whole-Cloth Wall Hanging

This 36" wall hanging is designed to include many aspects of both free-motion and machine-guided quilting. It has minimal piecing and is based on an Amish quilt. The piecing pattern is a medallion quilt with a narrow inner border and a wider outer border. The outer border is quilted in an undulating feather. The inner border is pumpkin seed. The medallion is a combination of grid and feathered wreath. This chapter shows one piecing version for the quilt top. The simple lines of the quilting can be used with a number of other piecing sets. The quilting pattern would look equally attractive on a whole cloth quilt of pastels, or midtone solids or on an Amish bar design. The medallion and set squares could be pieced as a square in square.

When choosing the fabrics, colors, and piecing patterns for your own version of this quilt, keep in

mind that dark fabrics conceal the quilting; light fabrics reveal the quilting. Another consideration is the quilting thread. High contrast colors will require invisible thread. Related colors can be quilted with a neutral cotton thread. The finer the thread, the less it will show. I suggest an extremely fine cotton thread called Cotona by Madeira. This fine thread comes in a limited range of colors and is perfect for heavily quilted quilts, like this whole cloth design.

Because of the number of simple pieces, this quilt is perfect for scrap fabrics. The largest piece is used for the backing, 1⅛ yard. The other portions require smaller pieces. The yardages state the exact amount of fabric needed for each piece or matching sets of pieces. You may choose to combine the side borders and corner squares to reduce the piecing and the fabric requirements.

PIECING DIRECTIONS

1. Construct the quilt top of your choice following the measured drawing and cutting directions in the chart, Whole-Cloth Wall Hanging Information, that follows.

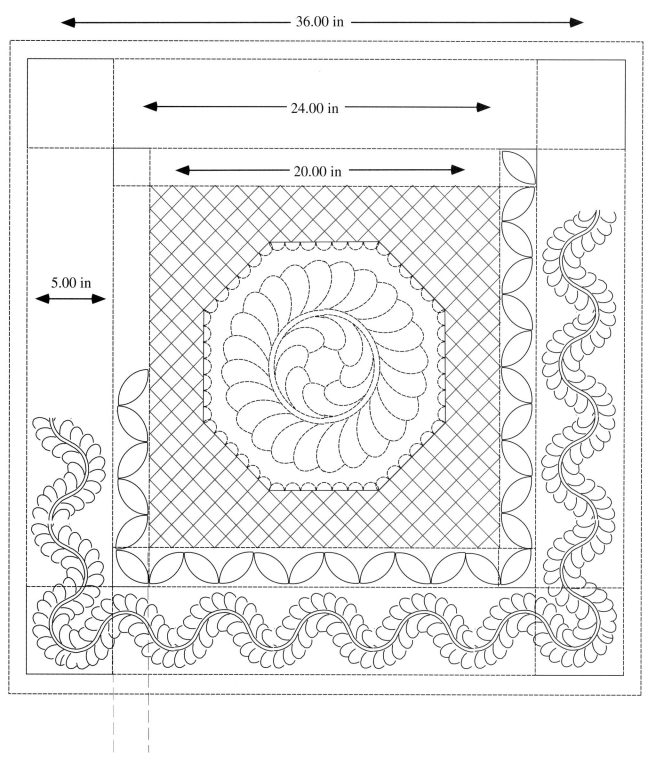

2.00 in

2. Mark the quilting design on the quilt top. I have mathematically designed the border pattern to fit as closely as possible to the quilt, but you may have to make minor adjustments as you mark the quilt. For information about fitting a border pattern to the quilt, see the quilting design hint, Fitting a Quilting Design to a Border, in the first chapter. The rectangle on the pattern highlights the repeat portion of the undulating feathers. The heavier dotted and dashed portion of the quilt indicates the join for the corner. Remember to stay within the inner 5" of the border. Do not draw in the outer

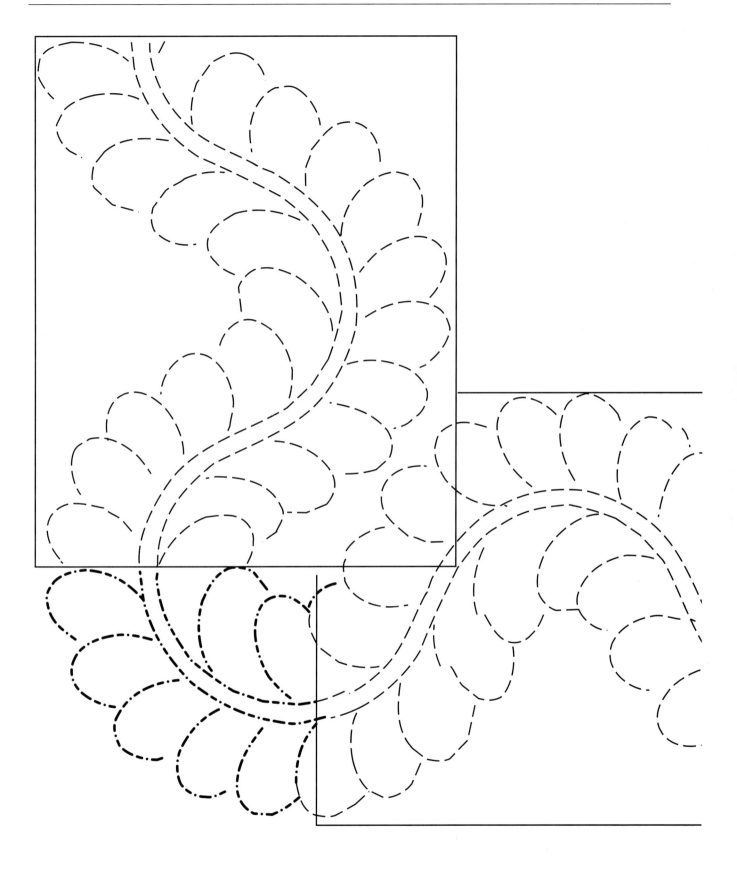

one inch that is allowed for straightening the quilt and adding the binding.

Look closely at the closeup of the pumpkin seed border. The corner block is slightly turned so both points are ⅛" from the outer edges of the border. There are ten pumpkin seeds on each side of the border and one in each corner. Notice the pumpkin seed doesn't touch the edges of the border. This makes the design easier to fit to the space.

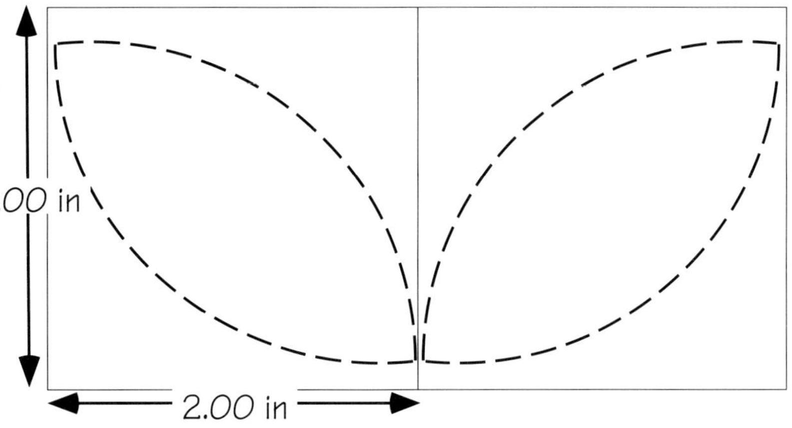

The quilt body is grid quilted with a ⅞" grid that measures 1¼" inch on the diagonal. The octagon in the center of the grid is determined by the size of the grid. The diagonal edges are six spaces long, while the vertical and horizontal edges are five spaces long. The circles on the inside of the octagon are ⅞" in diameter. You can mark these using a circle template available at office supply stores. This is an inexpensive plastic ruler that has dozens of different sized circles.

The pattern is given for the quarter feathered heart.

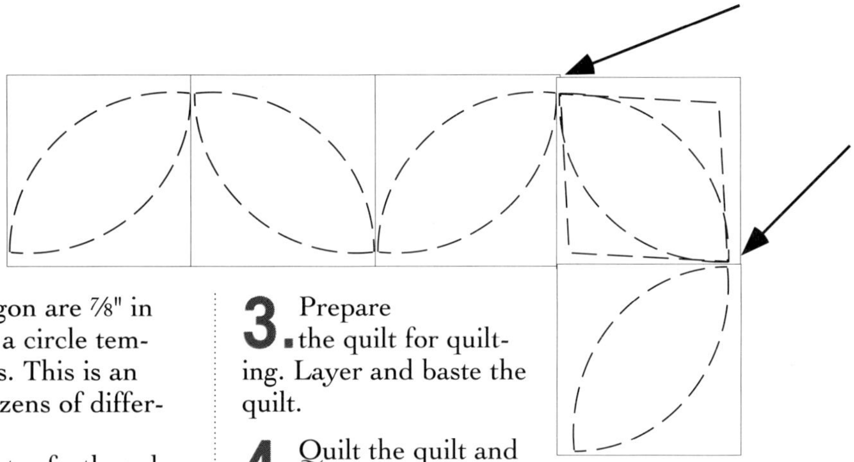

3. Prepare the quilt for quilting. Layer and baste the quilt.

4. Quilt the quilt and finish with ½"-wide French bias binding.

Whole-Cloth Wall Hanging Information

Amount of fabric required (in yards/inches)		Cutting Guide	
Inner medallion	20½" × 20½"	Inner border sides	2½" × 20½"
Inner border sides	¼	Total pieces	4
Inner border corner squares	2½" × 42″	Inner border corner squares	2½" × 2½"
Outer border sides	⅜	Total pieces	4
Outer border corner squares	6¼" × 42″	Outer border sides	6¼" × 24½"
Backing and rod pocket	1⅛	(There is an extra 1" on the width to allow for straightening the quilt before binding.)	
Binding	⅞	Total pieces	4
		Outer border corner squares	6¼" × 6¼"
		Total pieces	4
		Backing	38" × 38"
		Rod pocket	10" × 36"
		Binding (cut across the grain of the fabric)	6" × 42"
		Total binding strips	4

Chapter 7

QUILTING PATTERNS FOR BORDERS

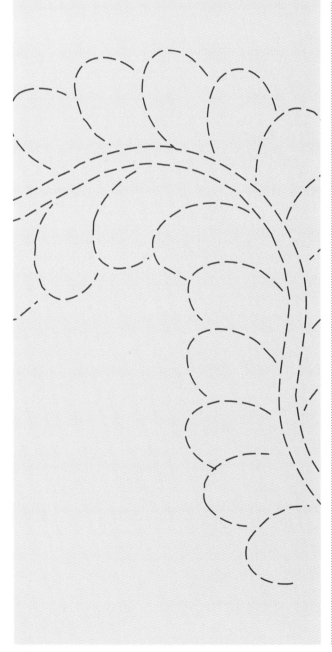

This chapter offers an assortment of designs and ideas for borders. It is important to choose a border pattern that reflects the style of the entire quilt. Borders are not an independent element, but part of a whole. They are like a great frame that enhances a great painting. The border pattern should complement the piecing pattern and the quilting pattern used on the quilt body. The type of patterns presented in this book lend themselves to low-key quilting patterns. Usually the designs are based on circles or straight lines and are so simple they don't require a pattern. The beauty of these quilts is in the piecing, and the border quilting should not detract from the quilt body. Another factor is the fabric choice for the border. Most of the quilts require a dark or printed border to act as a unifying frame around the multicolored piecing. The printed or dark border conceals the quilting, unlike plain, light-colored borders that reveal intricate quilting patterns.

A good choice for quilting borders is to follow the pattern in the print of the fabric. This is my favorite for border prints. There are usually straight lines and floral or curved motifs in border prints that can serve as a stitching guide. The straight lines can be done with the walking foot, while the floral or curved elements are done with free-motion quilting. This method is the simplest of the choices. It has the definite advantage of not requiring any marking. Usually this type of quilting is done with invisible thread, allowing the quilting line to cross any of the colors in the print. Another way to utilize print fabric in a border is to free-motion quilt around any of the motifs, even if the print is not a standard border or striped print. Common print elements are floral designs or novelty prints. These can be outlined and highlighted with lines of quilting. Or the border can be done in a large overall meandering pattern much like a large stipple quilting. This is fast, simple, and again doesn't require marking the quilting design. The only prerequisite to this free-motion quilting is to make sure the border is evenly quilted throughout. It is wise to plan ahead before starting to quilt. It is tempting to over-quilt the border at the start of the quilting, and become sloppy and rushed toward the end and under-quilt that portion. In a choice between under- and overquilted, I recommend underquilt. In most cases it is possible to put in a second line of quilting to fill out the design. The only exception to this is meander. How you begin is how you must end. It is a good idea to do a warm-up practice on scrap fabric to get the feel and look you are trying to achieve.

For many of the quilts I would recommend the border be quilted as an extension of the quilt body. This is done by simply extending the quilting lines into the borders. Two perfect examples are those piecing patterns done in grid or clamshell, like *Stars and Bars or Candy Swirl.*

Grid and clamshell are excellent choices for many of the borders. The straight line quilting of grid-based designs makes a plain graphic border that doesn't compete with the piecing. The grid choice can be hanging diamonds, or any number of channel quilt variations. Don't overlook the obvious rows of the straight lines that radiate out from the quilt body. These simple lines can be done with a walking foot and quilting guide. Grid Quilting, in the chapter Machine Quilting Update, gives instructions on how to mark a grid border. To add

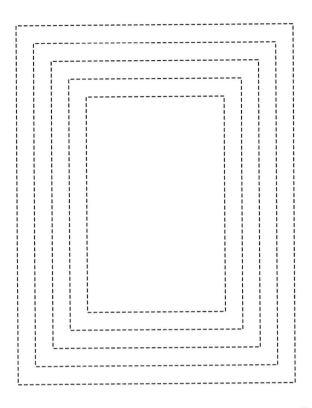

excitement to these straight line designs, try a small zig-zag stitch, a simple decorative stitch like the running stitch, or use a double needle.

Clamshell and its related curved variations including Baptist Fan, Pumpkin Seed and Cables are also great graphic designs. They give a softer feel to the quilt than the stark lines of grid or channel quilting. The half circle or partial circle forms the basis for the pattern; then other lines are added, mirroring the first line to fill out the design. Curved designs can pose a problem in resolving the corners. The large size of the curves doesn't leave any room for errors or adjusting of the pattern. There is a simple way around this problem.

To preclude the necessity for drafting the patterns to fit the borders and corners, I suggest ignoring the corner and running the designs off the edges (see illustration on the bottom of page 140). Symmetry is not an issue with this method. The designs start and stop at seam lines of the edges of the quilt without a thought about how the pattern fits the space. Usually I start marking the design in the center of the edge. In that way the two ends of the pattern are balanced and fall in the exact same place in the repeat. It gives the effect of careful planning without the work. This method is excellent for borders with butted corners. The abrupt ending to the pattern is justified by the seam across the border.

For an in-depth look at border patterns, I recommend *Quilting with Style Principles for Great Pattern Design* by Gwen Marston and Joe Cunningham.

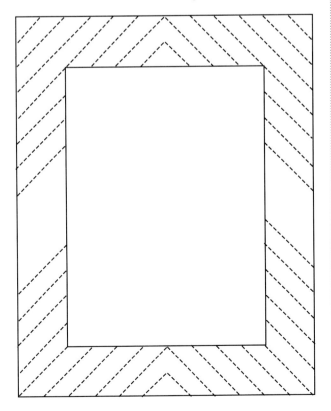

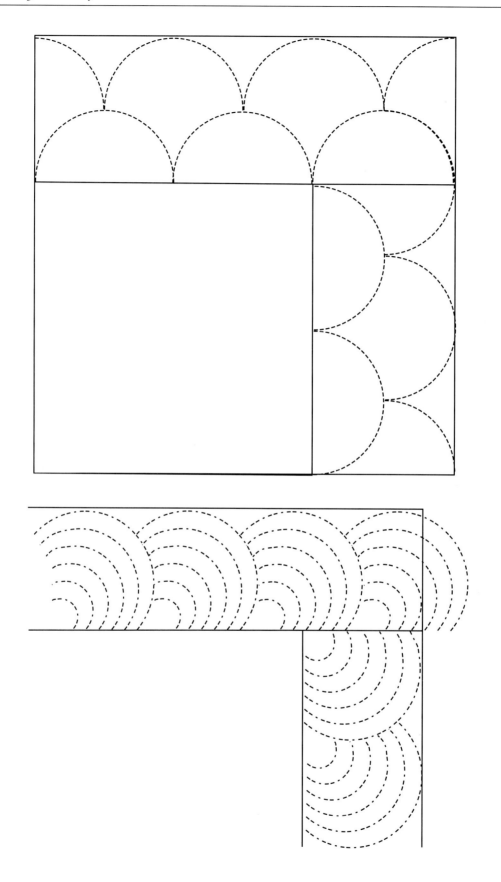

PART III
QUILTER'S SCHOOLHOUSE

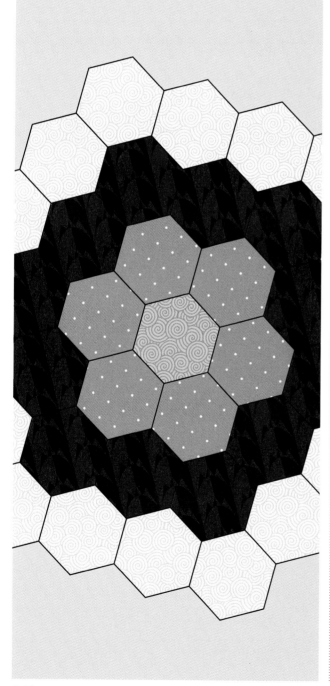

Chapter 8
FUNDAMENTALS OF QUILTMAKING

This is only an overview of basic quiltmaking techniques. For in-depth information, read my first book, *Teach Yourself Machine Piecing and Quiltmaking.*

Getting Organized

Equipment

Sewing Machine

The *sewing machine* is the indispensable tool in machine piecing and quilting. You need a dependable machine that sews a good-quality straight stitch on regular sewing or darning. Have regular maintenance on your machine to keep it in top-notch condition. It is important that you understand how your machine operates. At a minimum you need to know how to set your machine for straight stitch and how to adjust the stitch length. You should also know how to wind a bobbin, change a needle, change presser feet, and disengage or cover the feed dogs.

A number of presser feet are used in quiltmaking:

For basic piecing you may use a regular presser foot, a zigzag foot, a straight-stitch foot or one of the many ¼" presser feet available. No matter which foot you choose, it is important that you can stitch a true ¼" seam allowance.

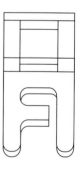

For advanced piecing you may choose to use an open-toe or no-bridge foot. The bridge of this foot has been removed to give an unobstructed view of the needle, the match, and the stitching line.

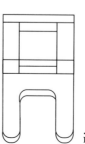

For quilting you may use a different set of presser feet. Use a walking foot for machine-guided quilting, and a darning foot or Big Foot

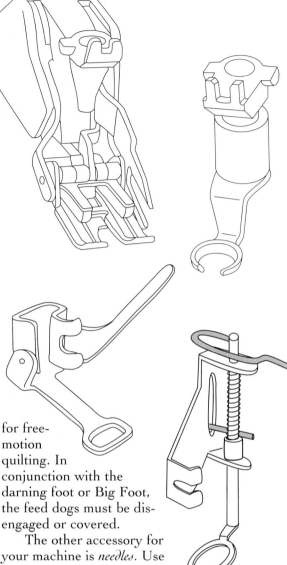

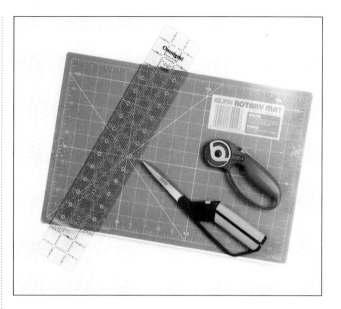

for free-motion quilting. In conjunction with the darning foot or Big Foot, the feed dogs must be disengaged or covered.

The other accessory for your machine is *needles*. Use sharp or universal point size 12(80) for piecing, size 14(90) for quilting.

Pressing Equipment

Steam iron. Choose an iron that steams evenly without spitting or staining. Use a commercial iron cleaner to keep the sole clean.

Ironing board. Use a firm pressing surface with a cotton cover.

Fabric Markers

Choose a *marker* that is accurate and easy to see. Fine-line pencil markers are best for piecing. Bold markers like water-erasable pens or chalk markers are best for quilting. Try out all markers on each piece of fabric in your quilt to insure they can be removed when the quilt is completed.

Cutting and Measuring Tools

Scissors. The scissors and shears should be sharp without catches. Make sure your scissors cut straight.

Rotary cutter and mat. Buy a cutter that has a safety shield to protect both the blade and you. Replace nipped or dull blades. Always use the rotary cutter with the special plastic mat designed for use with the cutter. It self-heals and is not damaged by the cutter. I recommend a mat with 1" grid marking. I also love the turntables designed to use with the mat. The turntable makes it easy to cut any shape, without moving the fabric on the mat.

Rulers. Choose a ruler with clear, easy-to-read markings that are visible on both light and dark fabrics. It should be marked in inches, quarter inches, and eighth inches. I prefer rulers that have markings in a grid. I recommend four sizes: 6" × 12", 6" × 24", a 12" square, and a 45-degree triangle.

Template Supplies

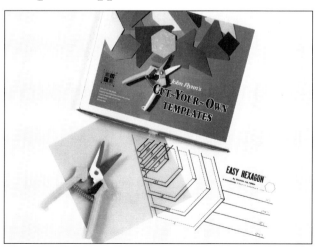

To make *reusable templates*, you will need clear or transparent template plastic. *Disposable templates* can be made of typing paper or lightweight cardboard (like manila file folders). You will also use a fine-line permanent marker and a $1/16$" punch.

For some patterns, Plexiglas templates are available. These templates/rulers are used with the rotary cutter. Hexagons and diamonds are common Plexiglas templates. You can have your own Plexiglas templates made at a plastics supplier, like Plastics To Go (see the Resource List). Having a custom-made template is not inexpensive, but it is a wonderful luxury when cutting curved or odd-shaped pieces.

A better alternative is using the rotary template making kit *Cut-Your-Own-Templates* by John Flynn. This kit includes rotary template plastic sheets and a cutter so you can make your own rotary templates.

Pins

Both *safety pins* and *straight pins* are used in machine quiltmaking. Straight pins are used in piecing and binding. Use long, thin pins with a large plastic or glass head. Safety pins are used to baste the quilt layers together for machine quilting. Size #1 nickel or brass pins are the commonly used size.

Safety pins should be stored open in a metal or plastic container. Leaving the pins open during storage reduces the amount of time it takes to pin the quilt and put the pins away after removing them from the quilt. It's a waste of time to open the pin to put it in the quilt, to close it to secure the quilt, open it to remove it from the quilt, and then close it to put the pin away. It is a lot less work to store the pins open.

Safety pins should be cleaned and sharpened before they are used. The pins are dirty from the manufacturing process and can have burrs or dull points. Clean and sharpen the pins with an emery strawberry. Emery strawberries frequently come with tomato pincushions. This small, strawberry-shaped bag is filled with sand. It is used by hand sewers to sharpen needles. Did you know there is a right and *wrong* way to use this accessory? If you have ever examined an emery strawberry, you know it is pliable. The sand shifts in the small bag. The emery inside is an abrasive like the emery on nail files or sand paper. The emery can only work when it is under pressure. To use the Emery Strawberry, insert the point of the pin into the strawberry. Press on the strawberry to compact the emery until it is solid. Rotate the pin point to sharpen and clean it. Then release the pressure on the strawberry and remove the pin.

Another pin accessory is the grapefruit spoon or Kwik Klip. These help to close the pins without breaking fingernails or getting sore finger tips. They both work on the same principle. The Kwik Klip is sold by quilting stores and the store owners will gladly show you the fine points of its use. The grapefruit spoon is sold at grocery stores and doesn't come with directions.

To use the spoon, insert the pin into the quilt layers. Don't close the pin. For right handed quilters the pin should be inserted so the pin is pointing to left. Take the spoon in your left hand grasping the handle. Scoop up the pin point with the teeth on the top right edge of the spoon. Twist your wrist to turn the spoon and raise the pin point. Grasp the head of the pin in your right hand and close the pin. The Kwik Klip is designed to close pins. It doesn't require a twist of the wrist and is kinder to both the wrist and fingers. I strongly suggest anyone with carpel tunnel syndrome use the Kwik Klip, not a grapefruit spoon.

Materials

Fabric

Medium-weight, closely woven, 100 percent cotton fabrics are the best choice for beginning quilting. Cotton fabrics are easy to press and sew. Common cotton fabrics are muslin, calico, gingham, and broadcloth.

Non-cotton fabrics like satins, silks, metallics, velvets, and cotton blends are suitable for many of the patterns. They add sparkle and interest to contemporary quilts. I am not discouraging the use of less traditional fabrics, but they may be more difficult for the beginner quilter to handle.

Threads

For piecing, use a fine, strong thread. One hundred percent cotton machine embroidery thread, size 50, is a good choice. One hundred percent polyester sewing thread or cotton-wrapped polyester thread are alternatives. Choose grey or beige thread for medium to dark fabrics, and white or off-white for pastels.

For quilting, the thread is limited only by your imagination. There are metallics, rayons, pearl cotton and many more exciting possibilities. For the beginner I recommend two types of thread: a fine sewing or embroidery thread to match the fabric, or invisible thread.

Batting

When choosing a batting consider three things: First, how much quilting do you want to do?

Polyester batting requires less stitching, while cotton or cotton-blend batting is better for dense quilting. Second, how much loft do you want in the finished quilt? Many antique quilts have low-loft cotton batting. The higher loft makes the quilt fluffy and thick. Extra heavy batts can look like feather comforters. Third, how skilled are you at quilting? The thicker the batting, the harder it is to handle. Beginners should stay with low-loft polyester or cotton-blend batting.

Basic Fabric Preparation Instructions

Prewashing

There are currently two schools of thought about prewashing fabrics. Not everyone agrees with the idea that all fabrics need to be prewashed. The most compelling argument for prewashing is the certain outcome of your finished quilt. There are no surprises when you have prewashed the fabric. When the fabric is prewashed, it removes excess dye and shrinks the fabric. On the other hand, because today's fabrics are made to strict specifications, shrinkage or bleeding are rarely a problem. Also, unwashed fabric doesn't require the tedious pressing required to straighten the wrinkled and tangled yardage that comes from the washer. I recommend that if you are not planning on prewashing your fabric, that you wash a 3" to 4" square of each fabric to test for shrinkage and bleeding.

Starching

Starched fabric is easier to cut, sew, and mark. A good coat of starch is the secret to great, trouble-free piecing. Starch also makes fabric markers easier to remove. There are four ways to starch the fabric.

1. The first method uses spray starch in an aerosol can or pump bottle. Spray starch is best for small pieces. To use spray starch: Mist the fabric with a coat of starch. Press dry with an iron on the cotton setting. Do not use steam. Repeat the process at least three times. Do not use this method for yardages. The method is the slowest and most wasteful. It uses a great deal of electricity for the iron, and the aerosol cans produce non-recycleable waste.

2. The second method uses a plant mister to apply the starch and permits the fabric to air-dry. Hang the dry-yardage on a clothes line. A mixture of 50% water to 50% liquid starch is sprayed on the fabric. Soak the fabric with the starch and let the fabric hang until it is dry. Repeat the process twice. Then steam-press to remove any wrinkles. This is my favorite method for most fabrics. Store any excess starch mixture in the refrigerator to prevent the liquid from mildewing.

3. The third method is used when prewashing the fabric. Liquid starch is added to the last rinse of the wash cycle. Follow the directions on the starch bottle for medium to heavy starch. After the final spin, remove the fabric from the washer and hang to dry. Steam press to remove the wrinkles.

4. The fourth method is to send the yardage to the laundry. Ask your laundry to treat your fabric like a tablecloth. Wash in cool water and use medium starch. Just think: no more handling and pressing yards of fabric rope! You may have to look around for a laundry that cares for your fabrics as you would, but it is well worth the effort. This is the method I most often use with large amounts of yardage.

Cutting Instructions

Template and Scissor Cutting vs. Rotary Cutting

Scissors and rotary cutters have different uses and advantages. Scissors are used for irregularly shaped pieces, usually the same pieces that require hand tracing around a plastic template. This method is slow but extremely accurate. Rotary cutters are best for straight lines and simple pieces. The rotary cutter is used with specially made rotary cutter templates or Plexiglas rulers, or with lightweight templates taped to a Plexiglas ruler. The pattern shape is not drawn onto the fabric. The ruler or template are simply placed on the fabric and used as cutting guides. The method is fast, but not extremely accurate.

Making and Using Templates

Templates are plastic or paper copies of the pattern that are used to trace the pattern onto the fabric. Lightweight plastic templates are used for pieces that require many repeats. The plastic template remains a constant size and doesn't fray or wear out during use. Paper templates are used for pieces that don't require many repeats, or for a cutting guide with the rotary cutter and Plexiglas rulers. Paper templates are fragile and can be used only a few times before having to be replaced.

To make a plastic template, trace the pattern, complete with cutting lines and stitching lines, onto a piece of template plastic. Use a permanent fine line marker and mark accurately. Cut out the template on the cutting line. To mark the match dots use a 1/16" punch.

To use the plastic template, place the template on the wrong side of the fabric. Trace around the template with a fine-line fabric marker like a quilter's silver pencil; also mark the matching points. Usually the template is drawn on a single layer of fabric. Place the pieces as close together as possible to conserve fabric. Use scissors to cut out the pieces.

To make a paper template, trace the pattern on a plain sheet of typing paper, or run a copy on a copy machine. If you are hand tracing the pattern, trace the pattern complete with cutting lines and stitching lines. If you use a copy machine, double-check the size of the copy against the original. Some copy machines distort the pattern. Cut out the template on the cutting line. Use the 1/16" punch to punch small holes in the template at the matching points. Mark each template with its pattern name, letter and grainline.

To use the paper template, layer two to four layers of fabric. Pin the paper template to the fabrics and use scissors to cut out the pieces. Mark the matching points on each layer of fabric.

Using the Rotary Cutter

The majority of the rotary-cut pieces in this book are based on the straight strip, the easiest and most basic of all cuts.

To make straight strips, begin by folding the fabric in half, selvage to selvage. Crease along the fold lightly with your hand. Fold the fabric in half again, lining up the fold and the selvages. You should now have four layers of fabric, about 10" to 12" wide. Use a ruler and right angle to square up

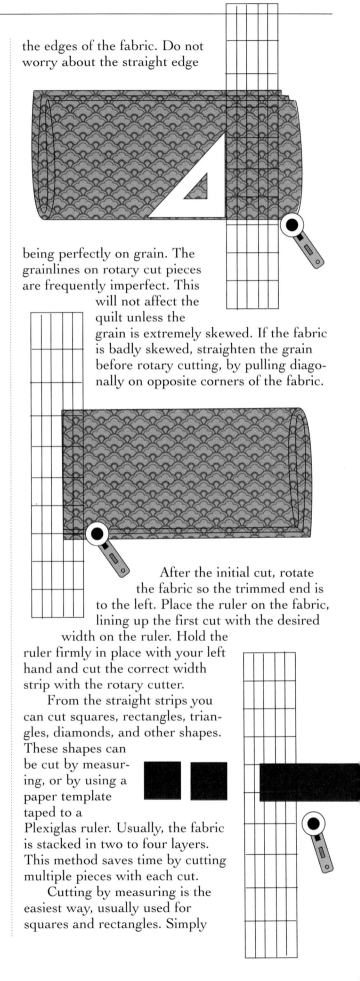

the edges of the fabric. Do not worry about the straight edge being perfectly on grain. The grainlines on rotary cut pieces are frequently imperfect. This will not affect the quilt unless the grain is extremely skewed. If the fabric is badly skewed, straighten the grain before rotary cutting, by pulling diagonally on opposite corners of the fabric.

After the initial cut, rotate the fabric so the trimmed end is to the left. Place the ruler on the fabric, lining up the first cut with the desired width on the ruler. Hold the ruler firmly in place with your left hand and cut the correct width strip with the rotary cutter.

From the straight strips you can cut squares, rectangles, triangles, diamonds, and other shapes. These shapes can be cut by measuring, or by using a paper template taped to a Plexiglas ruler. Usually, the fabric is stacked in two to four layers. This method saves time by cutting multiple pieces with each cut.

Cutting by measuring is the easiest way, usually used for squares and rectangles. Simply line up the ruler and cut. Triangles, diamonds and other shapes frequently use a clear plastic template.

Cutting by using a paper template is also easy. Tape the template to the wrong side of the ruler. Line up one side of the template with the edge of the ruler. Place the ruler over the fabric strip, lining up the template/ruler edge with the edges of the strip. Use your rotary cutter to cut the pieces. Quick cutting a diamond is shown in the illustration.

A third method uses custom templates for irregularly-shaped pieces. These templates are made from a heavy template material like Plexiglas or other heavy plastic that cannot be cut with the rotary cutter. For quilters accustomed to rotary cutting, these specialized tem-

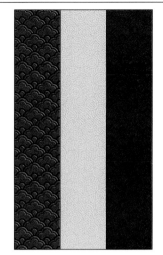

plates allow rotary cutting of any shaped piece with speed and accuracy.

Basic Piecing Instructions

Machine Set-Up For Piecing

Use an average length stitch, about 12 to 15 stitches to the inch or about a 2 stitch length on a metric scale. Have matching thread in the needle and bobbin. Use the basic ¼" presser foot for straight seams.

Seam Allowances

All the patterns in this book use a true ¼" seam allowance. To check your accuracy in stitching a true ¼", cut three strips of fabric 1½" wide by 6" long. Stitch the three strips together. Press the seams open and measure the width of the center strip. The center strip should measure exactly 1"

seam to seam on the right side. If it doesn't measure a true inch, repeat the steps, adjusting the way you feed the fabric.

Stitching the seams.

Stitch the seams from edge to edge when possible. Chain stitching is the fastest and most efficient way to sew. Do not break thread between pieces; simply feed a new set of patches under the foot upon completion of the previous set. The pieces will be joined by a short length of stitching. To use the patches, simply clip them apart. Backstitching or knotting the thread is not required for most designs. The notable exception to this is inset piecing, such as the diamonds in *Hexagon Stars* (see chapter 4). Inset seams start and stop ¼" from the edge of the fabric. The matching dots on the pattern are used as a guide to locate the ¼" from the edge of the fabric. To make an inset seam, start and stop sewing on the matching dot. Secure the seam with a few reverse stitches to make a knot.

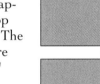

Pressing the Seams

Press with care and do not stretch or distort the pieces. Press with a steam iron on the cotton setting and move the iron in an up-and-down motion, rather than dragging it across the seam. Seams can be pressed towards the darker fabric or the seams can be pressed open. Both methods have advantages and often blocks have seams pressed with both methods. Pressing seams to one side is the fastest and simplest. It is the best choice for joining squares, rectangles, and curved seams, but the seams can be bulky. Open seams produce a smooth quilt top that lays flat. The open seams make matching points highly visible and difficult matches easier to see and correctly stitch.

Matching Points And Seams Accurately

The most basic match is straight seams that cross at a 90-degree angle. This match is called keying. Press the seams in opposite directions. Line up

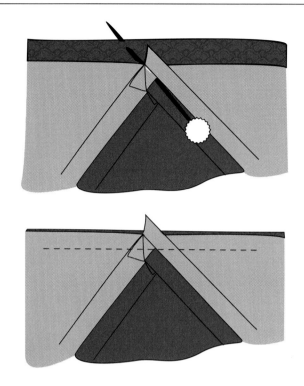

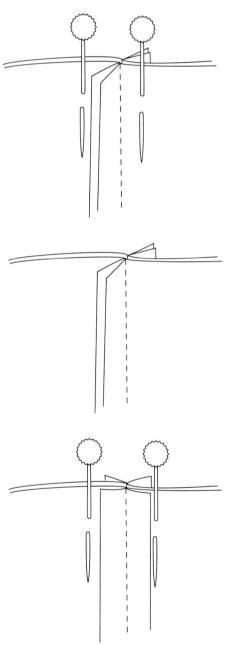

the matching seams and slide them together. The shallow rise from the opposing seam allowances help to form a perfect match.

Keying can be modified to work with seams that are pressed open. Tip the seams to one side and in opposite directions. Treat the match as a basic keyed match. Secure the match by pinning the block, *not* the seam allowances. This way the seam allowances can be stitched as open seams. Modified keying makes an easy, perfect match, and the open seams result in a flat block.

To match points like star centers accurately, use the stab-pin method. Skewer the matching points with a pin. Don't tip the pin

over or try to bring the point back into the fabric. Pin conventionally on either side of the stab pin. As you sew, tip the pin up parallel to the machine. Be careful not to pull the pin out of the fabric. Stitch right up to the pin and remove it as the needle secures the match.

Inset piecing is used where three seams come together, as in diamond- or hexagon-shaped pieces. Sew together the two pieces, bracketing the inset. Remember to stop sewing at the matching dot and backstitch two or three stitches. Press the seams open.

Line up the first edges, sewing toward the pressed open seam. Stitch toward the inset corner, across the open seam allowance. The last stitch before turning the corner should fall off the folded edge of the top fabric, as close as possible to the knot or backstitching. Stop with the needle lowered in the single layer of fabric underneath, the inset piece. Lift the presser foot, turn the corner, and line up the seam allowances. Lower the presser foot and continue sewing.

To join curved seams, sew with the concave curve on the top. (Concave curves inward. If you are having trouble remembering which is convex and which is concave, this lingo helps: Concave "caves" in.) Pin at the beginning and end of the seam. For large curves pin at the halfway mark of the seam. Stitch slowly. Stretch the edge of the upper piece to fit the lower curve. Use the point of a pin, or seam ripper to help align the seam allowances.

Adding Borders to the Quilt

The most common borders are butted and mitered. The butted border is the easiest. It is also the most casual-looking. I recommend it for beginners and for use with dark or printed fabrics. Mitered borders are more difficult. They usually require more fabric and a little more work. I recommend mitered borders for classic designs and on light fabric.

Butted Corners: Cut two border strips to match the measure of the long side of the quilt. To determine this measurement, measure the long side of the quilt body. Sew one strip to each of the long sides. Cut two border strips to match the measure of the short side of the quilt. To determine this measurement, measure the short side of the quilt body plus the two borders. Sew the two strips to the remaining sides.

Mitered Corners: The easiest way to make mitered corners is to sew the four border pieces to the four sides of the quilt, prior to marking the miter. The miter requires extra fabric in the corners. Cut the borders at least 1" longer than the finished width and lengths of the quilt. Do not cut the miters before stitching. Center the border strips along the four sides of the quilt body. Mark the four corners of the quilt body to indicate the ¼" seam allowances. The ¼" seam allowance is extremely important. Mitering borders require

inset seams. The stitching line for the borders starts and stops on the ¼" mark. Press the seam allowances open. Be careful not to stretch the quilt or borders when pressing.

The difficult part of mitered corners is obtaining a true 45-degree miter that lies flat. Incorrectly done, the borders can be too small for the quilt or the miters can be skewed. Surprisingly, there is a simple method that makes it almost "goof-proof." Lay the quilt, wrong side up, on a large flat surface like a table or the floor. The surface area must be large enough that at all four corners lay flat and smooth. That ensures the borders and miters are the correct size for the quilt.

Overlap the border strips. It doesn't matter which strip is on the top. Notice how the border strips overlap. There are short ends of the border extending beyond the edges of the quilt. These short ends mark the exact outside corner. Using a straight edge and fabric marker, draw a line from the outside corner to the inside corner. This will

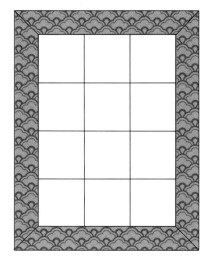

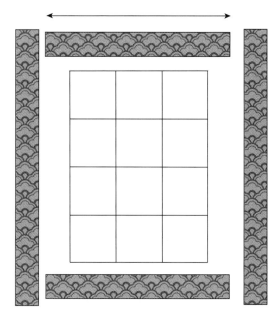

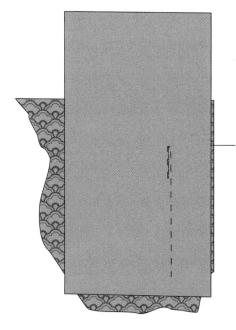

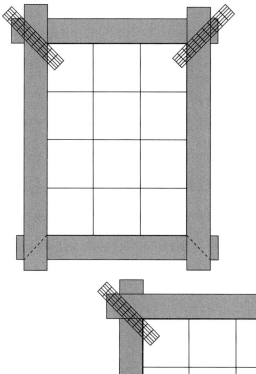

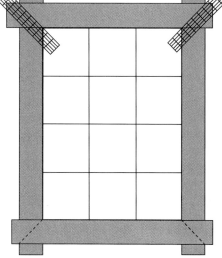

mark the miter on one side of the corner. Now re-layer the border strips, bringing the other border strip to the top. Mark this one as you did the first side.

You have both sides of the miter marked. To sew, put the borders right sides together. Use the marks to correctly line up the sides of the miter and pin the borders together along the miter lines. Stitch the miter, then trim the seam allowance to about ¼" inch. Press open the seams to complete.

Preparing the Quilt for Quilting

Marking the Quilt

Transfer the quilting design to the right side of the quilt top. Position the quilt over the paper pattern. For dark fabric use a light box to increase the visibility of the design. Trace the pattern onto the quilt. Begin marking at the center and work to the borders.

Basting the Layers of the Quilt Together

The three layers of the quilt must be held together during quilting. Stretching the backing before basting is a key step to obtain a smooth, unpleated backing. To stretch the backing, it needs to be securely taped or clamped to a table while you are basting the quilt.

Tape the backing, wrong side up, to a large smooth surface like a floor or table. Stretch the backing smooth and taut. If the backing is larger than the table, evenly drape the fabric over the table edges and secure the backing to the lip of the table with 1" binder clamps. Both the tape and clamps should be at about 8" to 10" intervals around the quilt.

Center and smooth the batting over the backing.

Center and smooth the quilt top over the backing and batting.

Baste the layers together on the stretched portion of the quilt. Use size #1 safety pins placed about every 4". Start pinning in the center of the quilt.

If the quilt is larger than the table, you will need to shift the quilt to continue basting. Remove the clamps from the backing by lifting the unbasted sections of the quilt to expose the backing and clamps. Remove the clamps being careful not to tear the backing. Slide the quilt until an unbasted portion of the quilt is on the table top. Stretch and clamp the three free sides of this portion of the quilt. Do not try to place clamps on the side of the quilt already basted.

Continue pin basting the quilt. Repeat the basic steps until the entire quilt has been stretched and basted.

Secure the Edges

Fold the backing over the batting and quilt front to make a temporary edge finish. This prevents the batting and excess fabric from being caught in the presser foot or being accidentally quilted to the back of the quilt.

Quilting Basics

Machine-Guided Quilting

Machine-guided quilting is the simplest form of machine quilting. Machine-guided quilting is like regular sewing. The machine does most of the work, including sewing straight with a perfect length stitch.

Machine guided quilting is used for straight line quilting like channel, grid, and stitch-in-the-ditch.

Use a walking foot for basic machine-guided quilting. Set the machine on straight stitch with an average stitch length. Start and stop each line of stitching with a knot. To knot, reduce the stitch length to almost zero for about four to six stitches. These tiny stitches make a secure, inconspicuous knot. Do this at both the beginning and end of every line of stitches.

To guide the fabric, use your fingertips to help evenly feed the fabric to the foot.

Free-Motion Quilting

Free-motion or free hand quilting is the most like hand quilting. The stitch formation, size, and location depend solely on the quilter's skill. It is excellent for intricate curved designs, like feather motifs. It is also used for background designs like stipple, echo, and clamshell.

Set up the machine for basic machine-guided quilting by choosing the darning foot or free-motion quilting foot. Disengage the feed dogs by lowering them or covering them. Set the machine on straight stitch with the stitch length at zero. The machine's stitch length doesn't affect the stitch length. The stitch size and place is determined by how you move the fabric.

Place the quilt on the machine where you wish to start. Lower the presser foot. Take one stitch and bring the bobbin thread to the quilt top. Hold on to both threads as you begin to sew. After a few stitches you can clip the thread tails to

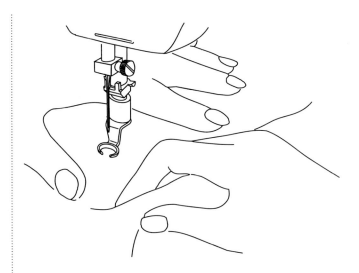

prevent them from being caught in the quilting stitches. To knot the threads make six to eight stitches very close together. Knot the beginning and end of every line of stitches.

To guide the fabric, cup your hands around the presser foot and lightly rest them on the fabric. Think of free-motion quilting as drawing. You are moving the fabric under a stationary pen (needle). Pull the fabric in the direction you want the stitches to move. Some designs require double stitching lines of the pattern. Try to duplicate the first line as closely as possible with the second line of stitching. Sew at a moderate speed. The stitches should be smooth and even—about the same size as the stitches in the machine-guided portions of the quilting.

Binding the Quilt

French Bias Binding.

There are a number of ways to bind a quilt. The most durable and professional-looking binding is a double-fold binding called French bias binding. It is made from bias strips cut from extra quilt fabric. The strips are cut six times the finished size of the binding. A ¼" finished binding would be cut 3" wide.

Making the Binding

Begin with the yardage required in the pattern or use one of the many charts available to help determine the yardage requirements. To cut bias strips, start with a square or rectangle. Draw a 45° angle across the fabric. Cut on this line, which results in two 45-degree triangles.

Join the triangles along the straight edges. Line up the straight edges of

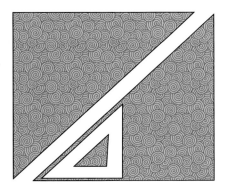

the two pieces as illustrated and sew them together with a ¼" seam allowance.

Mark the binding strips along the bias edge of the fabric and cut along the lines.

Stitch the bias strips together to make a single long length of bias. Fold the bias in half, length-

wise, wrong sides together and lining up the raw edges. Press carefully. Do not stretch the bias edges.

Binding Square or Rectangular Quilts with Straight Edges and 90-Degree Corners

Before binding the quilt, trim the quilt to the finished size (including width of the finished binding).

To start the binding make a bias fold. To make the correct fold, open the binding and place the strip wrong side up on the ironing board. Fold the end of the binding, bringing the top left corner to the right edge. Press the diagonal fold, and re-press the strip in half. Stitch the binding to the right side of the quilt. Line up the raw edges of the binding to the raw edges of the quilt. Begin stitching in the middle of a quilt side, not at a corner. Start stitching about 1" in from the edge of the binding to allow for joining the binding ends. The seam allowance should be

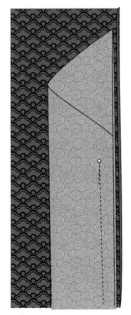

slightly less than the width of the finished binding. A ½" binding requires a ⅜" seam allow-ance.

To make a 90-degree mitered corner, as you approach the corner, measure ⅜" (or the seam allowance measure) in from the next side of the quilt and mark with a pin. Sew to the pin, back-stitch, remove the pin, and remove the quilt from the machine.

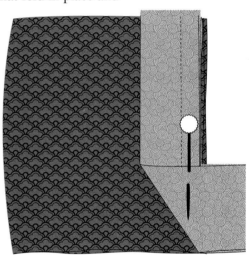

Fold the free end of the binding over the stitched binding. This will form a diagonal fold in the corner of the binding. Hold that fold in place and fold the free end of binding back onto the quilt, lining up the binding to the quilt edge. Resume stitching at the corner.

Continue around the quilt, sew to within 1" of the bias fold at the start of the binding. Back-stitch and remove the quilt from the machine.

Trim the free end of the binding to fit into the bias fold, overlapping the ends by at least ¼". Pin the join in place. Complete stitching the binding to the quilt.

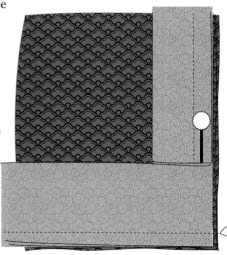

Turn the binding over the raw edges of the quilt to the back. Miter the back corners by hand to match the front corners. Hand stitch the binding to the wrong side of the quilt with a blindstitch.

Binding Quilts with Irregular Edges and 120-degree Corners.

Many of the quilts in this book have irregular edges. Usually there are two straight edges and two irregular-shaped edges. The corners on the irregular-shaped edges are both inside and outside corners and require special handling.

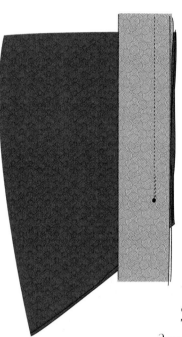

Before binding the quilt, trim the quilt to the finished size (including width of the finished binding).

Always begin the binding on the longest straight edge.

Fold and begin the binding as in the previous directions.

To make an *outside 120-degree mitered corner:* As you approach the corner, measure ⅜" (or the seam allowance measure) in from the next side of the quilt and mark with a pin. Sew to

the pin, backstitch, and remove the quilt from the machine.

Fold the free end of the binding over the stitched binding. This will form a diagonal fold in the

corner of the binding.

Hold that fold in place and fold the free end of binding back onto the quilt lining up the binding to the quilt edge. Resume stitching at the corner.

To make an *inside 120-degree mitered angle:* Place a pin at the exact inside angle. The pin should bisect the angle. Sew to the pin, backstitch, and remove the quilt from the machine.

Clip the seam allowance of the binding, not the quilt, to the last stitch. Turn the angle with the binding, pin in place, and continue stitching the remaining edges of the quilt. It helps to turn the angle if you tug slightly on the binding.

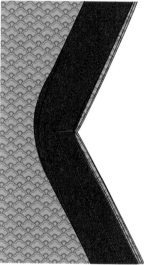

Continue around the quilt. Sew to within 1" of the bias fold at the start of the binding.

Backstitch and remove the quilt from the machine.

Trim the free end of the binding to fit into the bias fold, overlapping the ends by at least ¼". Pin the join in place. Complete stitching the binding to the quilt.

Turn the binding over the raw edges of the quilt to the back. Miter the back corners by hand to match the front corners. The outside 120-degree mitered corner is folded to the back and mitered like the 90-degree corner. The inside 120-degree mitered corner is more complex. Using an iron, fold the right side of the binding to form the miter. One side of the corner will fold under the other side. Press the miter in place.

Do not press across the entire width of the binding. Turn the binding to the wrong side and stretch the binding edge to make it lie flat. Usually the back binding does not have a crisp corner like the front binding. The back corner is more rounded and has less of a miter. Hand stitch the binding to the wrong side of the quilt with a blind-stitch.

Mock Binding

Mock binding is like facing the quilt edge. Its purpose is to attach prairie points without having to hand sew the edges of the quilt together. Mock binding is an unsuitable edge finish by itself. The binding is usually cut 1½" wide and will finish ½" wide.

Make a bias binding 1½" wide following the basic directions for French bias binding.

Before binding the quilt, trim the quilt to the finished size (including a ¼" seam allowance).

To start the binding, make a bias fold. To make the correct fold, open the binding and place the strip wrong side up on the ironing board. Fold the end of the binding, bringing the top left corner to the right edge. Press the diagonal fold, and re-press the strip in half.

Stitch the binding to the right side of the quilt. Line up the raw edges of the binding to the raw edges of the quilt. Begin stitching in the middle of the quilt side, not at a corner. Start stitching about 1" in from the edge of the binding to allow for joining the binding end. The seam allowance should be a scant ¼".

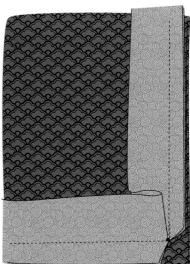

To make a 90-degree mitered corner, as you approach the corner, measure ¼" (in from the next side of the quilt) and mark with a pin. Sew to the pin, backstitch, and remove the quilt from the machine.

Clip the seam allowance of the binding to the last stitch. Turn the corner with the binding, pin in place and continue stitching the remaining edges of the quilt.

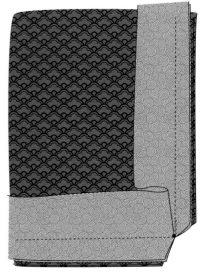

To end the binding, sew to within 1" of the bias fold at the start of the binding. Backstitch and remove the quilt from the machine.

Trim the free end of the binding to fit into the bias fold, overlapping the ends by at least ¼". Pin the join in place. Complete stitching the binding to the quilt.

To finish the binding, trim away the seam allowances at the corners of the quilt. Tip the binding to the wrong side of the quilt and press. Miter the corners and hand stitch the binding to the

MATH CHARTS FOR GRID LAYOUT

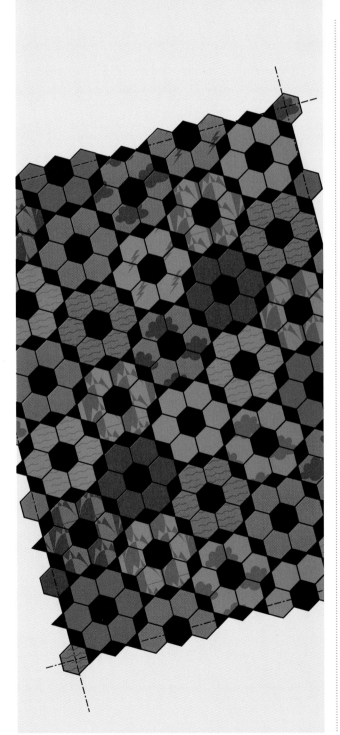

Diagonal grid measure

grid measures	on the diagonal
½"	¾"
⅞"	1¼"
1"	1⅜"
1½"	2⅛"
2"	2⅞"
2½"	3½"
3"	4¼"
3½"	5"
4"	5⅝"
4½"	6⅜"

Repeats Guide
(calculated to fit a 24" ruler)

½" grid

¾"	1 space
1½"	2 spaces
2¼"	3 spaces
3"	4 spaces
3¾"	5 spaces
4½"	6 spaces
5¼"	7 spaces
6"	8 spaces
6¾"	9 spaces
7½"	10 spaces
8¼"	11 spaces
9"	12 spaces
9¾"	13 spaces
10½"	14 spaces
11¼"	15 spaces
12"	16 spaces

⅞" grid

1¼"	1 space
2½"	2 spaces
3¾"	3 spaces

Repeats Guide
(continued)

5"	4 spaces
6¼"	5 spaces
7½"	6 spaces
8¾"	7 spaces
10"	8 spaces
11¼"	9 spaces
12½"	10 spaces
13¼"	11 spaces
15"	12 spaces
16¼"	13 spaces
17½"	14 spaces
18¾"	15 spaces
20"	16 spaces

1" grid

1⅜"	1 space
1½"	2 spaces
2¾"	3 spaces
4⅛"	4 spaces
3¾"	5 spaces
5½"	6 spaces
6⅞"	7 spaces
8¼"	8 spaces
9⅝"	9 spaces
11"	10 spaces
12⅜"	11 spaces
13¾"	12 spaces
15⅛"	13 spaces
16½"	14 spaces
17⅞"	15 spaces
19¼"	16 spaces
20⅝"	17 spaces
22"	18 spaces
23⅜"	19 spaces

1½" grid

2⅛"	1 space
6⅜"	2 spaces
8½"	3 spaces
10⅝"	4 spaces
12¾"	5 spaces
14⅞"	6 spaces
17"	7 spaces
19⅛"	8 spaces
21¼"	9 spaces
23⅜"	10 spaces

2" grid

2⅞"	1 space
5¾"	2 spaces
8⅝"	3 spaces
11½"	4 spaces

Repeats Guide
(continued)

Repeats Guide *(continued)*

14⅜"	5 spaces
17¼"	6 spaces
20⅛"	7 spaces
23"	8 spaces

2½" grid

3½"	1 space
7"	2 spaces
10½"	3 spaces
14"	4 spaces
17½"	5 spaces
21"	6 spaces
24½"	7 spaces

3" grid

4¼"	1 space
8½"	2 spaces
12¾"	3 spaces
17"	4 spaces
21¼"	5 spaces
25½"	6 spaces

3½" grid

5"	1 space
10"	2 spaces
15"	3 spaces
20"	4 spaces
25"	5 spaces

4" grid

5⅝"	1 space
11¼"	2 spaces
16⅞"	3 spaces
22½"	4 spaces
28⅛"	5 spaces

For grid sizes larger than the chart, the diagonal is easy to determine. The formula is: the width of the grid × 1.41 = the diagonal measure. For example, multiply 1½" (1.5) times 1.41. That equals 2.115. To make that number easy to measure, round it off to the nearest eighth of an inch—2.12 or approximately 2⅛". The 1½" grid has a diagonal measure of 2⅛".

The repeat measurements are easy to calculate. They can be multiplied or done with addition. I usually do the repeats for the 24" ruler. As in previous steps I round the decimal to the nearest eighth of an inch.

PIECING HINT

Use Calculator with Repeating Addition: I use a calculator that keeps repeating the addition. For example to find the repeats of 2⅛", I press in 2.125 + 2.125 then press the plus key (+) again and get 4.25. Pressing the plus key a third time shows 6.375. Every time I press the plus key, the total is increased by 2.125. It's painless math.

Decimals for every 1/16 inch
(to help translate calculator numbers to ruler fractions)

1/16	.063
1/8	.125
3/16	.188
1/4	.25
5/16	.313
3/8	.375
7/16	.438
1/2	.5
9/16	.563
5/8	.625
11/16	.688
3/4	.75
13/16	.813
7/8	.875
15/16	.938

Resource List

This list of businesses is by no means a complete list of all the reputable quilting stores or mail-order businesses. It is a list of those businesses I have dealt with and found to be courteous and helpful.

The Cloth Cupboard
P.O. Box 2263
Boise, ID 83701

Carries many quilting notions including thread, fabrics and batting. This is my source for the 1/16" punch.

Clotilde Inc.
1909 S.W. First Ave.
Fort Lauderdale, FL 33315

Clotilde specializes in sewing notions for all types of sewing— markers, scissors, cutters, patterns, rulers, and pressing aids.

Nancy's Notions
Dept 2564 P.O. Box 63
Beaver Dam, WI 53916

Nancy's carries a large selection of sewing notions, including thread, cutting tools, rulers, pressing aids, markers and other sewing notions.

Keepsake Quilting
Route 25B, PO Box 1618
Centre Harbor, NH 03226-1618

Keepsake carries a large selection of quilting supplies, including books, patterns, fabrics, rulers and cutting tools. They offer fabric medleys (the fabrics are matched for you.)

Quilting Books Unlimited
1158 Prairie
Aurora, IL 60506
Phone (708) 406-0237

Specializes in books, books and more books. Its ad states it has every quilting book currently in print, and after dealing with them, I believe it. It is a book buyer's dream.

FQFC-M
100 Shiloh Overpass Road
Billings Montana 59106

The Flynn Quilt Frame Company manufactures the John Flynn's Cut-Your-Own Templates kit that includes cutting shears, 4 sheets of template material for making your own rotary templates, and instructions.

Quilts and Other Comforts
Dept 25050272
1 Quilters Lane
Box 4100
Golden, CO 80402-4100

Wide selections of quilting supplies, including books, patterns, and fabrics, also markers, rulers, and cutting tools.

Plastics to Go
6050 Nathan Lane N.
Plymouth, MN 55442
(612) 551-1140

This is my source for Plexiglas products including the extruded bar I use for marking grid quilting.

Index

Profile of the Author

By Robbie Fanning, Series Editor

Deb Wagner has assured her place in machine-quilting history at a young age by winning the 1993 and 1995 Bernina Awards for Best Machine Workmanship at the American Quilting Society show in Paducah. Her quilts were also honored with first place awards in 1989, 1990, and 1991 in the Traditional Pieced category.

Each quilt she makes is characterized by exquisite, copious, precise machine quilting and unexpected machine piecing of odd angles and curves. One judge told me that the jurors could not find one thing wrong, front or back, with her 1993 winning quilt.

How does Deb do it? How did she develop the machine skills? How does she develop an idea?

She answers, "My ideas for quilts come from one source: the past. Since childhood, I have been enchanted with the past, especially the late 1700s to the early 1900s. For high-school graduation, I asked for a spinning wheel; for college, a cylinder record player—not your normal gifts!

"For me, the past is an endless source of ideas, from quilts, lace work, embroidery, folk art, even knitting patterns. I collect historical books about all types of textiles, pottery, home furnishings, painting, and jewelry. I also have hundreds of costume and fashion books. I have all the *McCall's Needlework and Crafts* magazines since the 1920s and quilting patterns from the late 1930s. In general, I hoard books and papers and a lot of other things. My house is in danger of sinking into the ground from 12 clocks in my sewing room, 1000 seashells, and a growing collection of 1930 to 1950 pottery."

From these many sources, Deb pulls a border here, a block there, until she has the elements for a design. "I know the type of quilt I am most comfortable making: formal block setting, intricate piecing (circles and triangles) or appliqué (flora and fauna), with lots of quilting. From there, I am drawn to ideas by shape and color. I also want a certain feel for every quilt. This is more difficult to define. Something indefinable speaks to me—a season, a collection of shapes, the way the sky looks on an August night, poetry or a quote. Each design represents more than just lines and shapes."

How does she develop these ideas into the quilt? "The ideas seem to bubble up. I'm blessed with a good memory for where I saw an idea, so I keep mental track of those I found most interesting. When the ideas really grab my attention, they move up to the next level of importance. I photocopy them and add them to file folders and notebooks. Each file is on a specific idea or theme. It may contain patterns from other sources, references to other books or magazines, color and fabric choices. When I decide to make a new quilt, I go to the file and choose the quilt that most appeals to me.

"Usually, a collection of ideas/elements for a quilt are posted on the walls of my workroom and bedroom. I look at the ideas for months before beginning the designing. Mentally, I try out all the variations I can think of, adding elements, rearranging portions. I study and rework ideas dozens of times before the actual physical work begins.

"From the time I am first inspired by an idea till the time it becomes a workable quilt can take anywhere from one to two years. The idea board for the 1993 Bernina quilt, *Floral Urns*, hung on my walls for over a year and was in my files for a year before that. The current quilt has been on the idea board for two years and will take two more years until it is a completed quilt.

"I only like working on one or two major quilts at a time. I don't work fast. I'd rather do one huge, impressive quilt than five quick quilts."

Once the quilt is scheduled, Deb makes detailed drawings, using the computer and copy machine. This becomes the working pattern, containing all the measurements, color choices, fabric types, and logical progression of work. "I do all the design work before I make the first cut. I don't let the quilt or the process take control of the finished product; I always know what I'm going to get at the end of the process. It may seem structured, but I don't have time to waste on quilts that may fail. For me, it's just as exciting and fulfilling to design the quilt in my mind as to play with the fabric—and it's cheaper and more efficient! I love the mental workout. It's a form of meditation: relaxing, engrossing, enlightening."

Deb has a vast fabric stash. "When I see something that has the look I want, I buy it instantly. My favorite colors are a golden yellow, bright red, orange, watermelon pink, and indigo blue. I recently spent $500 in 30 minutes at Hancock Fabrics in Paducah. I know what I like and what I want. I don't waste time looking at fabrics that won't work in my quilts."

Deb's machine skills come from helping her parents in their sewing-machine store. At age 9 she was demonstrating the machines—and selling a lot. She sewed as she grew up and has known she wanted to be in the textile field since she was 16. She has a BA in Clothing, Textiles, & Design from the University of Wisconsin at Stout. Later, she moved back to her home area in Cosmos, Minnesota, and, along with family members, bought a farmhouse outside town, complete with more than 45 cats.

Her sewing studio and office is 17' × 22', with east and north exposures ("important in the dreary north country"). She has three large tables in the sewing area. One is for cutting, one is for whatever current machine she's using, and the third is a giant 36" × 60" glasstop table. "It's perfect as a light table for full-size quilts. It was a wonderful $40 buy at a local flea market, but it weighs a ton. It took three people to get it into my second-floor studio."

While she works, Deb plays a wide assortment of music, from Baroque to Beach Boys. Because her job encompasses teaching internationally, fulfilling commissions, writing, and making quilts, Deb leads a work day as structured as any other working person's. "I work from about 9 am to 5:30 pm, six days a week. I think it is very important to maintain a schedule. In fact, there is some medical proof that maintaining a time table can lengthen one's life span. In my free time, I walk, garden, refinish furniture, and go to estate sales and auctions. (This is my Achilles' heel. I can't pass up a garage sale, Salvation Army thrift store, flea market, or household auction.) At the end of the day, I relax, read, and meditate.

"I have come to realize that very few people can honestly say they are doing the work they have always dreamed of and planned for. I feel so lucky— I've met wonderful people, traveled more than I ever dreamed I would, seen my work win awards and acclaim. I'm also frequently frazzled, upset, and overworked. But I know I have an enviable measure of happiness.

"I have a phrase on my wall above my desk that sums up my feelings about my work:"

One cannot eat all day, or sleep all day,
or make love all day, every day for the rest
of one's life. The only pasttime one can
pursue hour after hour, day after day, is work.
It is work that makes us who we are. The way
to happiness is to discover the work you love to do.